Purpose Seekers

Jackie Flemming

To: Lillie
Be Blessed!!

Jackie
Flemming

Purpose
Seekers

The journey
of your life
begins here

Jackie Flemming

T&J Publishers

First, I would like to thank my Lord and Savior, Jesus the Christ, for all of his blessings. I can't imagine my life without him.

Secondly, I would like to thank my husband, Timothy Flemming, Jr. He is so creative, so inspiring, and so wonderful to me. I want to thank my kids, Timothy Flemming, III; Timera JaNae Flemming, and Jeremiah Flemming for being three of the best kids any parent could have. God has blessed me with all three of them.

And lastly, to all of my friends, family, loved ones, and supporters, thank you for your prayers and support.

Pur·pose: "The reason for which something is done or created or for which something exists."
Seeker: "Someone making a search or inquiry."

A purpose seeker is someone who seeks God to discover why they were created and what they were designed to be and do in life.

"For I know the plans I have for you. They are plans for good and not for disaster, to give you a future and a hope."—God (from Jeremiah 29:11, New Living Translation)

TABLE OF CONTENTS

FOREWORD

*T*HERE ARE SOME THINGS MONEY CAN'T BUY—
purpose is one of those things. The beautiful
thing about purpose is: it lies beyond the in-
visible border of human potential and ability. It doesn't
matter how smart you are—or think you are. It doesn't
matter where you are in life: wealthy, poor, famous, in-
famous, unknown, hailing from an affluent household,
from the ghetto, from a successful family; or from a
family of thieves, addicts, and troublemakers. Everyone starts at the same place along this journey: the spot
where human ability ends and God's ability begins.

There is nothing more fulfilling than living out
your purpose. There is an internal void automatically
built into every man's soul that can only be satisfied by
knowing God and His purpose for our lives. Money can't
fill it. I know we've been told otherwise—that money is
the key to happiness. Well, tell that to the many celeb-
rities who can't seem to drink enough, party enough,
club enough, rendezvous with strangers enough; shop

11

for new clothes, houses, and cars enough to satisfy their appetite for life. One famous NBA basketball player has three luxurious mansions, but he hardly sleeps at either of them. He's barely home because...Stucco, hardwood flooring, painted walls, fancy wallpaper, marble counter-tops, lazy boy chairs, and plush couches situated in front of decorated fireplaces with flat screen televisions positioned above them always lose their luster after a while. New car smells fade away. Two hundred inch flat screen televisions can't eliminate the redundancy of the television programming that is being played on them. New Gucci bags and Red Bottoms can't speak an assuring word or a word of consolation to you in the midnight hours. There's a need to be held by someone, a need to connect on an emotional and mental level with someone, a need to feel important, so you look for Mr. Perfect or Ms. Perfect only to find out that artificial intimacy leaves you just as empty as that new dress you bought but forgot was hanging up in the closet—with the tag still on it. Material things don't last. Only that which we do for Christ provides us with lasting fulfillment. God is eternal, and His presence satisfies to the utmost, quenching the thirst of our eternal spirits. That is why Jesus told the woman at the well the water He provides is the only water that can quench our eternal thirst—that we would never have to drink another cup after taking just one sip.

This is where your journey begins. This is where you take off the grave clothes of false identity that have kept you bound for so long in the dark tomb of uncertainty, and you run towards the light of your God-given destiny with a new zeal, new life, new assurance, and an unshakable confidence. It doesn't matter how you got to this point—of holding this book in your hands. What matters is you're here. And you're not here by accident or coincidence either. God is calling you to a higher level of living, a life teeming with purpose and lasting satisfaction; he's calling you to a life destined to outlive you.

Embrace the journey. Accept the call. Let God reveal to you his purpose for you, his plan for your life, the path he has carved out just for you in the vast forest of time.

—Timothy Flemming, Jr.

PURPOSE SEEKERS

INTRODUCTION

WOULDN'T LIFE BE SO MUCH EASIER if the moment that you come into the age of accountability someone hands you a road map for your life that lists all of the details: where you should go, what you should be when you grow up, where you should attend school, who you should marry, etc.? That would be great. You'd feel confident enough to make decisions without hesitation. Regrettably, I must inform you that life is not that simple. Being that we are free-will agents (meaning God doesn't make decisions for us, but we are given the freedom and responsibility to make decisions for ourselves in life), there is always a degree of uncertainty lurking in the back of our minds when it comes to many of life's decisions. Sometimes people will ponder "What if..." in their minds: "What if I attended another school, picked up another major, chose another career path, married someone different, etc.?" Yes, uncertainty can rob us of our confidence in decision making; it can hinder us from pursuing certain paths; it can thrust us into a state of panic, and even depression. But there's one decision that will never backfire on us: the decision to trust God with our lives and follow his Spirit where ever he leads us. The only thing that guarantees us true success and fulfillment is living a Spirit-led life.

God lets us choose whether or not to follow him and his will. He told his people in the desert to make a decision whether or not they wanted life or death, blessings or curses. He even suggested—God doesn't force anything on us; he simply suggests to us what paths we should take—to them to choose life. At some point in my life I grew tired of moving in destructive circles, engaging in self-destructive habits, and I changed my tune. I made the decision to follow God. There's a song that I like to sing. It's an old familiar hymn which simply says, "I have decided to follow Jesus. No turning back. No turning back." I made that decision in June of 1998, at the age of 16. It was at a youth conference held at my church. At the time I was simply visiting the church and didn't think God had me on his mind, but that night God spoke directly to me through the message given by the speaker and I found myself running to the altar with tears in my eyes, desperate and ready for God to give me a new life during the altar call. I'm a living witness that God sees and thinks about us more than we know, and that he can reach us no matter where we are.

I was only 12 years old when I was introduced to a lifestyle of sex and drugs. Today, I'm a product of someone else's prayers. I had plans for my life, but God messed my plans all up when I was sent back to Sumter, South Carolina to stay with my grandmother. She was a powerful prayer warrior and mother at a small Pentecos-

tal church. She would pray all over me daily and fa
my brother and I. Whenever she'd go to church, we had
to go also. I couldn't even sneak a blunt or a cigarette
into her house because the Holy Spirit would always let
her know when I had one...before I even arrived at her
house. She was a prophetess. She'd see right through me.
I can honestly say today that my grandmother changed
my life. She'd pray off demonic spirits that would attack
me in the midnight hours. She'd come into my room at
night, sit in a chair, and speak in tongues all over me. I
would feel so much peace when she was present.

When God is trying to get your attention he has
a way of sending people into your life to help you. Without my grandmother, I would probably still be trapped
in the bondage of Satan. I'm sure there are some people,
or at least a certain someone in your life today, who God
has been, and is using, to lead you to himself. All of us
have those people: whether it be a parent, grandparent,
a friend, a loved one, work colleague, a missionary God
may send to your door one Saturday morning, a school
teacher, or a television or radio personality. If we're honest, we can all admit that we do have positive influences
in our lives; many of us just ignore them.

For a season, God sent me to live with my grandmother in South Carolina; however, seasons do come to
an end. Later, I was sent back to Atlanta to live with
my aunte. My grandmother's health was beginning to
fail. I planned to go to my old crowd once I got back to
Atlanta. I wanted to go back to the lifestyle I was accus-
tomed to before going to live with my grandmother, but
God had other plans. My aunt, who came and got me
and my brother, was also a praying woman. She served

17

faithfully in the church I now attend. She took me that night in June to that youth conference where God got my attention. God was pursuing after me even though I didn't desire him at the time. He wanted to show me a better way. He wanted to rescue me from a bondage I didn't know I was in. I thought sex and drugs was the way, but God knew that those things were leading me down a path of destruction I would never make it back from had he not caught me in time. God was leading me to himself so that he could introduce me to a life I would truly love. I wouldn't have to pretend to be happy while secretly living in fear. I wouldn't have to hook up with guys who left me in an even lowlier state than I was in before I met them. I recently saw some of my old friends and noticed how nearly unrecognizable they are. Their bodies have been ruined by the drugs and alcohol we use to consume, and they look much older than they are. All I could think was, "That could have been me." God has blessed me beyond my wildest dreams. I have the husband of my dreams: a wonderful man who loves me with the "love of the Lord." I have three wonderful kids. I feel great mentally, and emotionally; and I'm in the right place spiritually. I have real peace, real joy, and the assurance of my future. I had to make a decision to say *yes* to God. He chose me, but I still had to choose him; and if you are reading this book, that means God is calling your name just like he did mine.

2 Peter chapter 3 reveals to us that God is patient towards us. He waits for us. He doesn't give up on saving and delivering us. It doesn't take years and years and years to be set free and have your life placed on the right path; it does, however, take some people years and

years to surrender to God. They think they have time... although no one knows how much time they have left on this earth. They're listening to the enemy (Satan) who's promising them the world, while forgetting that it profits us nothing to gain the world and lose our eternal souls. But if you're still alive, there is still time. It doesn't matter where you are right now. What matters is that you surrender to the one who designed and created you, the one who loves you unconditionally, the one who has the perfect plan for your life, the one who said in Jeremiah chapter 29 that his plans are to bless us and prosper us and not to curse us; surrender as I did to Christ Jesus. With Jesus, you don't need a road map because... he is the way, the truth and the life. He's waiting. I'm here as his vessel to guide you to him and to teach you how to receive that which he has for you.

Everyone has a story to tell, but I want to know, "Which path are you on? God's or yours?" If you don't know, then you will discover the answer in the pages of this book.

As you go through this book, you will need your journal close by, as there will be some exercises you will need to complete. We are going to uproot some hidden things, drop some destructive attachments in our lives, and allow the Holy Spirit to map out a new strategy for us as we take this journey together. Habakkuk 2:2 says, "Write the vision, and make it plain..."

Let us begin.

PURPOSE SEEKERS

CHAPTER 1:
WHERE IS "HERE"?

*T*HE SMELL OF THE APARTMENT REEKED of weed and alcohol; it was dirty and filthy. Outside the room where I was there was a line of guys waiting—at least ten of them. I didn't know any of them. All I knew was they were all waiting for their turn with me. In the next room my friend lay. One after another boys were having their way with her. I could hear them laughing after they were done, joking about how her baby was going to look like all of them. Fortunately, my menstrual cycle came on after the first guy, allowing me to be spared from the hands of the rest. My friend was not so fortunate though. Although there were at least ten to twenty guys upstairs in that apartment with us in the Grady Homes projects, I could hear scores of others entering into the apartment, all of them lured by drugs, alcohol...and two runaway teenage girls they had picked up earlier at the mall: my friend and I. They fed us, but also expected us to have sex with each of them while there. The concept of freedom became an illusion at that point. We were stuck. Scores of pistol carrying, weed smoking, alcohol guzzling, thugged-out guys were all around us, and we knew we weren't going to simply walk out of that apartment unscathed. The main question that crossed my mind while I was considering my predicament was: "How did I end-up here?"

Before I found myself in such a horrible situation—facing rape, possible disease, pregnancy; and perhaps, even the loss of my life—there were certain decisions I made that led up to it. The Bible says the "wages" of sin is death in Romans 6:23; and in James chapter 1, James tells us that certain of our decisions can lead us into sin, and sin always culminates in death, both spiritually and physically. I was dead spiritually, and possibly facing the other death; and it was all because of me, because of my choices. I chose to run away with my friend that day. I chose to follow a group of guys back to an apartment that day. I put myself in that circumstance. Both my friend and I started out chasing after boys and ended-up trapped by strange men.

We were fortunate to get out of that apartment that day simply because my friend, who was pregnant at the time, needed food. So, the guys, unwilling to bear the burden of a pregnant teenage girl, let us leave. We had to go back home and face the music: the police report that had been filed for missing persons; our parents who were in a state of panic and extreme stress; the serious damage we had dealt to those closest to us. What selfish and reckless actions we took. But all of us, without knowing it, have been, or are stuck in a place we don't need to be when outside of God's will. The panic my mother felt can only be rivaled by the pain and grief God feels when his creation, man, is kidnapped by sin and dragged to a burning hell. You may not be in an apartment surrounded by a group of thugs, looking like a lamb surrounded by wolves; but you may be in a relationship that's destroying your life, a career that's destroying your family, a cult that is leading you further into deception, an addiction that is controlling you and robbing you of a future; in a state of mind that is dangerous, pondering suicidal thoughts or thoughts of depression; in an adulterous relationship, in a jail cell, a prison cell, sleeping behind an abandoned building, in a tremendous amount of debt that's siphoning all of your money week after week, in a state of bitterness, malice, jealousy, envy, hatred, un-forgiveness, and demonic bondage; and ultimately, Satan's plan for you is that you die and end-up in the one place no person in their right mind would want to be: hell. To die in a state of sin is to end-up in the flames of hell—and yes, hell is a real place that Jesus talked about. In fact, Jesus talked about hell— the place where "the worm never dies" and there is continual "weeping, wailing and gnashing of teeth"—more than he did heaven in the gospels. He obviously realized that more people are in danger of ending up in hell than in any other danger. Hell is where Satan wants all of us to end-up. Hell is eternal. In light of eternity, your job, career, education, degrees, money, fame, friends, family, and all of your material possessions holds no value. You can't take any of these things with you into the afterlife. Make your soul's salvation your number one priority. Let being in right standing with God through Christ be your number one goal, not money and material things.

I'm reminded of a parable Jesus gave in Luke chapter 12, starting at the 16th verse. There, the Bible says, "A rich man had a fertile farm that produced fine crops. He said to himself, 'What should I do? I don't have room for all my crops.' Then Jesus said, 'I know! I'll tear down my barns and build bigger ones. Then I'll have room enough to store all my wheat and other goods. And I'll sit back and say to myself, 'My friend, you have enough stored away for years to come. Now take it easy! Eat, drink, and be merry!' But God said to him, 'You fool! You will die this very night. Then who will get everything you worked for?'" Then Jesus concluded with this important statement in verse 21: "Yes, a person is a fool to store up earthly wealth but not have a rich relationship with God" (New Living Translation). Of all of the places you don't want to end-up, being in a state of separation from God due to sin is the worst. It's better to be killed while in a relationship with Christ than to die peacefully of old age while not knowing Christ. Comfort is a bad place to be in. Many people today might not be dealing with drugs, promiscuity, alcohol, and other vices, but they are addicted to their comfort-zones, and they don't realize that life— God's life, which he wants to give to them—is passing them by. It profits us nothing to gain the world and lose our souls. The world may even know your name, but does God know you? It's better to be popular with God than popular with the world. You're not going to make it into heaven just because you're a celebrity or a superstar. That stuff means nothing to God.

You must ask yourself, "Where am I, and how

did I get here?" if you're going to discover God's purpose for your life. I was chasing boys, but are you in a spiritually dangerous place in your life today because you're chasing money, material things, validation and acceptance from people, and fame? You can lose all of those things in the blink of an eye, even your life. James said life is like a vapor: here one minute; gone the next. Nothing is promised to you outside of Christ. This is why you can't replace God with a spouse, a child, money, or a career. These things are good, but in the blink of an eye you can lose them all; and then you will only be left with...God. Everything begins and ends with God; in fact, it's all about him. There are no short cuts around God. In the end, you'll eventually be completely alone, staring him in the face, and it's at that point that you'll either hear him say, "Well done my good and faithful servant" or "Depart from me you worker of iniquity, I never knew you."

Not everyone ends up in a dangerous place by choice. In our nation today there is an epidemic of human sex-trafficking, there are brothels where young girls are being held against their will; there are children lost in the foster care system, suffering at the hands of child molesters and cruel guardians; there are children and adults who are in places they don't—and shouldn't—want to be. But the most dangerous place to be in is outside of Christ and his will. Even if you're in a bad place physically, Christ can see and rescue you if you call on him. The Bible says God's eyes are over the righteous and his ears are open to *their* prayers in 1 Peter 3:12. When the Bible tells us all things work together for the good of them that "love God" and are "called according to his purpose" (meaning they have aligned themselves with God's plans and purpose for their lives) in Romans 8:28, that doesn't mean everything that happens to God's people is good or a part of God's perfect will; what it does mean is God can—and will—invade our situations and cause them to work together for our good. The most important thing is to know where you are spiritually; that's the beginning point of transformation. All else flows from there.

GOD'S QUESTION TO YOU

In Genesis chapter 3, God, after seeing that man (Adam and Eve) had fallen from grace and had hidden themselves, asked Adam, "Where are you?" God knew where they were physically—after all, he sees everything. God was asking a rhetorical question (a question he already knew the answer to). In fact, he was probably looking right at them when he asked them the question. God wanted Adam and Eve to examine where they were spiritually. Where are you? Are you in God's will? Are you serving God's purpose? Are you truly in a relationship with Christ? Or are you stuck in a spiritual bondage surrounded by demons waiting to rob you of your spiritual inheritance? How can you discover the answers to these questions? By examining the condition of your heart using these questions:

1. *Have you given up your desires and plans for the desires and plans of God?* Don't say, "I don't have any plans." Everyone has plans. If you just want to loaf around, smoke weed and get drunk everyday, that's a plan. If you just want to play video games and eat pizza everyday, that's

a plan. You're making decisions everyday of your life. Doing nothing is still a decision. But have you sacrificed your plans and desires in exchange for God's? Have you made the decision to live for him instead of for you?

Jesus said, "If any of you wants to be my follower, you must turn from your selfish ways, take up your cross daily, and follow me" (Luke 9:23, NLT). Selfish desires, the desires of the flesh, sinful desires, worldly desires (being more focused on pleasing and living for the world than for God), the desire to make your name great (rather than seeking to make God's name great), the pursuit of riches (Proverbs 23:4 says we're not to labor to be rich. God will bless us when our hearts and motives are in the right place), and the pursuit of power and prestige (Jesus said the greatest among men is the servant, the one who's humble enough to put others before themselves, not the one that tries to look and act big, in Matthew 23:11) are all desires we must abandon. You can't find God's purpose while living for yourself.

2. *How much are you sacrificing for God?* Do you give God time in the morning and throughout your day? Do you seek him before making decisions? Do you do the simplest thing the Bible, in James chapter 4, tells us to do: ask God what is his plan rather than assuming you know his plan or assuming you know what to do? James wrote, "Look here, you who say, 'Today or tomorrow we are going to a certain town and will stay there a year. We will do business there and make a profit.' How do you know what your life will be like tomorrow? Your life is like the morning fog—it's here a little while, then it's gone. What you ought to say is, 'If the Lord wants us

to, we will live and do this or that" (vs. 13-15). Making plans without praying is dangerous. We're to go to God first and ask him if he wants us to do x, y, and z, or what he wants us to do.

A lot of people don't want to seek God for his will because it entails sacrificing time—television time, radio time, club time, etc. It also entails sacrificing sinful pleasures, since John 9:31 explains that God ignores the prayers of sinners and listens only to the prayers of those who're "worshipers and doers of his will" (the only prayer God will receive from a sinner is a prayer of repentance, a prayer asking for salvation). We can't expect God to bless us while we're living in disobedience to his word. These two things—sin and time—are the things most people are unwilling to give-up in order to spend time with God. The flesh always fights against the Holy Spirit (Galatians 5).

In Psalm 37, the psalmist says, "Take delight in the Lord, and he will give you your heart's desires. Commit everything you do to the Lord. Trust him, and he will help you" (vs. 4-5, NLT). The word "delight" here means "to be soft, be delicate" in the Hebrew language. This means: Be soft in God's hands, soft enough for him to mold and shape you; surrender to him and don't fight against him, against his will, against the convictions of the Holy Spirit; don't argue with his word and try to live the way you want to while trying to get him to endorse your plans. Be soft in his hands. Let him shape your life. The more you surrender to him, the more he will shape your life into that which he desires; the more he'll transform your heart and mind so that you desire and seek after that which he intended for you to have from the beginning. And when your heart has been changed as a result of fellowshipping with him, then God will give you the desires of your *new* heart—he'll transform you so that you'll desire the right things.

Remember: Prayer is not a useless exercise, it is not something you suppose to do only when you're in trouble, it is not some spooky activity that you as a Christian have the option of participating in, and it certainly isn't a function designated only to a certain group in your church (the intercessory prayer team). The Bible says we, as Christians, must "pray without ceasing" (that means never stop praying). We are to bring every "prayer and supplication" to God in 1 Peter chapter 5. We are to "live by faith" according to Romans 1:17. Jesus said we must not live by physical bread alone, but by "every word that proceeds out of the mouth of God" in Matthew 4:4. So, the life of a Christian is a Spirit led life, one in which they pray and hear the voice of God—and do what he instructs them to do. Without a prayer life, you cannot be a Christian, and you cannot hear and receive from God. You can't have a relationship with someone you don't communicate with; therefore, how can you expect to have a relationship with God if you don't have a prayer life?

WHERE GOD WANTS YOU TO BE
Now that I got you thinking about where you are spiritually, let me now reveal to you where God wants you to be. In Psalm 91, God says,

"Those who live in the shelter of the Most High will find rest in the shadow of the Almighty. This

I declare about the Lord: He alone is my refuge, my place of safety; he is my God, and I trust him. For he will rescue you from every trap and protect you from every deadly disease. He will cover you with his feathers. He will shelter you with his wings. His faithful promises are your armor and protection. . . . If you make the Lord your refuge, if you make the Most High your shelter, no evil will conquer you; no plague will come near your home. For he will order his angels to protect you wherever you go. . . . The Lord says, 'I will rescue those who love me. I will protect those who trust in my name. When they call on me, I will answer; I will be with them in trouble. I will rescue and honor them. I will reward them with a long life and give them my salvation'" (vs. 1-4, 9-11, 14-16).

God's desire is for you to reside in his presence so that he can protect and bless you. His promise of protection and blessings isn't given to everyone, just those who love and trust him. So, come out of the place of darkness. Get out of that place of spiritual, mental and emotional bondage. If you want to do so, you can start by praying the prayer below.

PRAY THIS PRAYER:

Heavenly Father, I thank you for your precious son, Jesus the Christ. Thank you for sending your own son to die in my place on the cross, to shed his

---

blood for my sins. Forgive me for my sins. Wash me with the blood of Jesus. I surrender my life to you. I surrender my plans to you. I surrender my heart, mind, body and soul to you. Do with me whatever you desire. Give me a clean heart and the right spirit. Let my desires line up with your will. For, today I choose to seek after your will, not mine. I denounce the world, and I denounce sin in my life. Sin no longer has dominion over me because now I am your child. No longer do I choose to pursue after the things of the world, and to be drawn away from you. Holy Spirit, fill me and draw me closer to you. Let my heart hunger and thirst for you like never before. Let my heart burn with a passion to know you, and long for you like a deer desperately longing for water. I surrender today. Thank you, for I receive this knew hunger and thirst by faith. It's in Jesus name I pray, Amen.

PURPOSE SEEKERS

CHAPTER 2:
THE SOURCE OF PURPOSE

*I*HELD A PARTICULAR VIEW OF GOD prior to learning the truth about him. In my mind growing up, I viewed God as a boring character who presented a ton of rules; these rules being put in place to rob me of my fun. I figured I would wait until I got older—much, much older—to get saved. By then I would have settled down, grown too old to do many of the things I used to; maybe my joints would be too weak, my bones too frail to "drop it" anymore; maybe arthritis would have set in and I would be incapable of moving about like I used to. Then, and then only, would I surrender my life to God. I didn't think God deserved my youth, energy and vitality. I didn't realize that tomorrow wasn't promised to me either. I just assumed I had plenty of time.

Maybe you were told as I was that by surrendering to God at a young age you would be "missing out" on life. That's what I believed; that's also what drove me into the devil's trap. I figured God may have had a plan for me, but his plan was boring, dull...and suitable mainly for older people. I had to learn the hard way that by serving the flesh I was missing out on true living; but I didn't know back then. No one told me the truth: that serving God is actually fun, and that by serving him I wouldn't have to be plagued by so many problems.

When I was younger I idolized people like Lil' Kim, the famous female rap artist whose music was laced with the most extreme, explicit, and sexually degrading lyrics. I liked the way she dressed and presented herself. You have to understand that in my neighborhood, the things that were idolized were promiscuity, drugs, gang-banging—all of the things that would make you popular. All I saw were hookers, strippers, and video girls, parties and cookouts every week (many of these girls claimed they couldn't find money for food to feed their children, but they could find money for alcohol and drugs to bring to these cookouts) that usually ended in fights and even shootouts. No one was talking about church, heaven and hell, doing positive things, college or sports. Sometimes, in an effort to fit in young people will embrace trends in their community. I wanted to be known as a promiscuous girl like Lil' Kim. The frightening moment came when a much older man came to me after finding out who my idol was, and he asked me if I would do all of the things Lil' Kim talked about in her songs. That's when the reality that I really didn't want to be that type of person sunk in. However, like many young people, I tried to portray myself as something I really wasn't, and it won me attention I was not ready to handle; attention I was unwilling to receive.

I let my surroundings dictate to me my purpose and shape my identity. I also listened to opinions about God coming from people who didn't know God. If they said God was boring, then I believed that God was boring. Many people formulate opinions about God based off of hearsay rather than God's word and experience.

The devil loves to play with our minds by planting distorted perceptions in them. In Genesis chapter 3, he played with Eve's mind by planting a seed of doubt and suspicion in it. All he had to do was plant a seed, and Eve did the rest. Satan went to Eve and whispered in her ear that God was trying to hide something from her. Notice: Satan never tried to get Eve to follow him; he was simply trying to get her to abandon and distrust God. The enemy will speak words into your ears to taint your spirit and distort the way you see God, yourself, and life. Who told you that you were ugly? Who told you that you were stupid? Who told you that church is boring and lame? Who made you think and feel that way? Whoever it is, they lied.

Satan had a clever trap set for me. Death looked so beautiful to me back then. Sin seemed so fun back then. I mean, today I can tell you that most of the popular girls—"freaks" they were regularly called by the guys attracted to them—have STDs, have multiple children by multiple guys who lend them no support while they struggle as single parents living off of the government (welfare), can barely find work because they lack the basic skills to maintain a decent paying job, are addicted to drugs and alcohol, and are dead before their time; but I didn't see it then. I didn't realize that what Satan depicts as fun is really poison; that it's really an illusion.

There's nothing fun about STDs, liver poisoning due to alcoholism, broken homes, unwanted pregnancies, drug addictions, or laying in a ditch somewhere. I thought smoking weed was the funnest thing in the world until I found myself being rushed to the hospital after smoking pure marijuana. My heart was racing too fast, my head was spinning, and I was slipping into cardiac arrest. I was literally on my deathbed! That's not fun. If we were to open our eyes, we'd see that these are the things sin brings us; this is the great deception Satan uses against us to keep us locked in generational curses and destructive patterns. This is why Jesus said he came that we might have life, and that we might have life more abundantly in John 10:10. And just before he made that statement, he said "the thief" (Satan) comes only to "still, and to kill, and to destroy." God promised us that his blessing (favor) makes us "rich" and "adds no sorrow" in Proverbs 10:22. What drug dealer do you know can boast that they don't have to look over their shoulders every second, worried about the Feds, police, or other dealers who want to knock them off; or that they don't deal with troubled consciences due to the many people they hurt just to get a dollar? How many strippers do you know that really enjoy degrading themselves for money in the strip clubs? Sin not only destroys the body, it destroy the mind through guilt and shame. That's why so many people hide from God, feeling as if they're not worthy to be used by him or even loved by him.

Not everyone grew up in the same type of environment as I did. Some people grew up in a completely different type of environment, but are equally as lost as I was. For example, look at the rich young ruler from

Matthew chapter 19: he was young, wealthy, successful, and morally upright. When Jesus confronted him with the commandments of God, this young ruler stated that he kept them all from his childhood up. But Jesus challenged him in the area of his bondage. You see, although he had everything anyone could ever want in life—he had the success, the wealth, the proper upbringing, good manners, influence, the education, and even the exposure to religion at an early age—what he didn't have was the freedom to walk away from all of these things and serve the living God. He was actually a slave to his environment—even though his environment was a positive one. He felt important and validated because he had accomplished everything *man* told him he needed to accomplish in order to be somebody; but sadly, he was lost. He wasn't a slave to drugs and promiscuity; he was a slave to money and status. His purpose was given to him by his surroundings. He noticed that he was missing God (despite being religious), but was enjoying his status too much to surrender to God. Money and status shapes many people's identities and supplies their sense of purpose. There is a lyric by a holy hip hop artist named Flame that stands out to me. He stated in one of his songs: gaining success "may get you out of the trap, but there's a sin problem much bigger than that." Social status can't change the fact that you are a sinner who is lost and in need of salvation; that sin has robbed you of a relationship with the God who gives us true purpose. It doesn't matter where you go; you carry sin with you.

There's another man in the Bible whose sense of purpose was shaped by his environment rather than God—and this man was devoutly religious: in Luke

15:25-32, there is the story of the prodigal son's return to his father's house; but the emphasis of this passage of scripture is on the oldest son, the one who didn't backslide and venture out into the world. This son represents individuals in the church who think they are righteous because of what they don't do. They think that because they stayed in the house (representing the church) they own both God and the church. They have taken on an identity formed by a religious environment. It is simply their tradition to go to church. They sing in the choir and serve on auxiliaries, dance, shout, pay tithes, etc., but like the oldest son in Luke 15, their hearts are full of jealousy, envy, self-righteousness, strife, and arrogance. Many people today are joining the church, but are not joining Christ; they are religious, but not really saved; they have a relationship with the pastor, but not the Savior; they know how to shout, but not how to worship; how to sing hymns, but not how to surrender; how to dance, but not how to fellowship with the Holy Spirit; even how to operate in spiritual gifts, but not how to walk in God's love; church is their identity, and church people provide for them a sense of purpose. If they don't get the attention they seek from the pastor or from other church people, they lose their joy, their peace, their ability to praise God. It was never about God; it was always about them and the validation they receive from men; they live for it. And when they see others stepping into office, they become insecure...like the older brother who felt threatened by his younger brother's return—as if *baby brother* was going to steal his shine.

You know your sense of purpose comes from the wrong things when you only feel important with these things. If you're not in a office, or don't have a title, then you don't feel necessary or obligated to do anything. This is the danger of the religious bondage: many church goers are looking for significance only in positions and titles, and they don't want to be who God called them to be and do what God really called the church to do: pray, intercede, lift up a standard of righteousness in society, witness to the lost, make disciples of Christ by teaching others to "observe" everything Christ commanded us to do, and engage in spiritual warfare. Very few, if any, prioritize things like prayer services, performing outreach activities, and interceding for the lost (a call given to every Christian. God never designated prayer to a special auxiliary: the intercessory prayer team).

You also know your source of purpose is something other than God when you feel as if you can't survive without "it"—whatever "it" may be. That "it" is your idol. The rich young ruler's "it" was his money. Some people's "it" is their career, job, house, car, image, family member, position, title, and even their accomplishments. Anything you cannot let go of is an idol in your life. You'll end-up being controlled by these things. God will always challenge you to let go of your idols before he blesses you because he doesn't want you to look for an identity and a sense of purpose in anything other than him.

My "it" at first was my status in the hood. Later on, my "it" became my job. Working as a leasing agent for a big property management company, I felt really good about myself. I was making good money, and felt as if I had reached a certain level of success due to my income. But God later gave me a challenge: he challenged me to quit my job. He closed the door in my face to excel in the company after challenging me to step out on faith into my own business, which was his will and purpose for me. What idol is keeping you from your God-given purpose?

EXERCISE:

Take a moment and examine yourself. I want you to make a list of the things in your life you feel you can't live without, things that make you feel significant and important. What is your "it"? I want you to make this list in your Purpose Seekers journal under the section "My hidden idols." Be as real and honest with yourself as possible. We are going to denounce these idols at the end of this chapter.

RECEIVING YOUR PURPOSE FROM THE RIGHT SOURCE

Jesus, in Matthew 10:39, said, "He that findeth his life shall lose it: and he that loseth his life for my sake shall find it." He reiterated the same words in Matthew 16:25 where he said, "For whosoever will save his life shall lose it: and whosoever will lose his life for my sake shall find it." In that same passage, Jesus told us that we must take up our "cross" and follow him if we're to be his disciples. What was Jesus saying? He was teaching us that our true purpose comes from him, and that only by giving up our goals and dreams for his can we discover what God wants us to be and do in life.

Some who claim they want to know their purpose are not really interested in knowing the purpose of God; they simply want God's material blessings, but not the work that comes with his will and purpose for them. The purpose of God is his task for your life, not the house and car he wants to give you. When you ask God for his purpose, you're asking him to give you your assignment task. Is your assignment to be a missionary in Africa, a missionary in your community, a witness in your neighborhood or on your job, to clothe the naked and feed the hungry while sharing the gospel at home or abroad? Is God's assignment for you to take the gospel to Hollywood, the addicts on the streets, the prostitutes on the corners, to the Grammys, or to the market place?

The "cross" is all about the sharing of the gospel. So when Jesus said you must abandon your goals and pick-up your cross, he was saying you must stop focusing on money, status, a big name, fame, and stop looking for security and comfort, and you must make reaching the lost your priority. Place your priorities, motives, and intentions in the right place before God speaks to you about the life he wants you to live. This is hard to do for many because, like the rich young ruler, they feel as if giving up the world's riches and security just to follow Jesus while he travels around preaching the gospel is too risky. Some even argue with God, claiming that they'd be better witnesses for him if they didn't have to make the sacrifice he is challenging them to make; but God knows us better than we know ourselves, and his plans aren't the same as our plans for ourselves. My husband, before entering into the ministry, was an amateur boxer. He didn't want to enter into the ministry because he thought that he would have had a bigger platform to represent God from had he become a celebrity fighter—he'd have more influence; however, the boxing ring was not God's plan for his life; the pulpit was. I thought that by being a top model I would have more influence to use to impact the lives of others with; so, when God spoke to me and gave me my assignment I told him that I wasn't able to do the things he asked me to because I had not yet achieved the status the world deems important, I had not yet reached the level of success needed to do what God was calling me to do. That was my way of thinking, but God's ways aren't our ways. He doesn't call the qualified; he qualifies the called. He opens doors for us as we step out on faith and obey him, not before we commit to obeying him. It starts with our commitment to fulfilling his will, which is to win lost souls for Christ. If your motives are geared towards *self*, then God's purpose is not for you. You must abandon *self* if you're going to walk in God's purpose for you.

Now, I'm not telling you to quit your job and pray all day. The Bible did say in 2 Thessalonians 3:10 that if we don't work, we don't eat. Don't make hasty decisions without first hearing from God. What I am telling you is: if God speaks to you about making a sacrifice, do it. Let go of what he tells you to let go of. Leave whatever he's telling you to leave. Do as Abraham did and abandon whatever God tells you to walk away from when he speaks to you. This is how it works: First, in order to hear from God, you must abandon your sin. In Hebrews 12:1, God tells us to "lay aside every weight, and the sin which doth so easily beset us" so that we may continue on the path God has placed us on. He told us to abandon our "sin" (what sin or sins are you clinging on to today?) and "weight" (a weight is not a sin, but an activity that leads us into sin. For example, going to certain clubs is not a sin, but that type of environment will lead you into sins like fornication, getting drunk, and entertaining demonic music). When you take the first step and do this—or, as James chapter 4 says, "draw nigh to God"—then God will "draw nigh to you" and speak to you concerning the next step or phase of his will for your life. That next step may be him telling you to quit your job and step out into a certain business, leave the city where you live and go to another state, start up a ministry, marry a certain individual, etc.

God speaks to us in phases. He never shares all of his plans up front. You have to obey the first instruction he gives you before he shares with you the second. God doesn't give us the whole plan up front because we would get ahead of him rather than relying on him. We would rely on the flesh to bring about something only God can bring about. We'd rely on our cunningness and ability rather than *walk by faith* (wait for God to speak to us). And worse: we would attempt to walk into blessings we are not prepared to handle. You see, along the process of obtaining God's will we must not only release those things around us which are a hindrance, but we must also get things out of us that hinder us from obeying God. That means some of us must get rid of some strongholds (ungodly thought processes): pride, a poverty mentality, welfare/entitlement mentality, carnality, wrong perspectives about relationships based on things like pornography and bitter advice from others who have had failed relationships, insecurity, a controlling spirit, misconceptions about God, un-forgiveness, selfishness, the desire to prove something to people in order to receive their validation, a victim mentality, a fascination with sin, and religious bondages such as self-righteousness and a works-based salvation. The devil wanted me to think God and church were boring so that he could keep my mind blinded to the truth of God's word. The devil didn't want me to discover who I am in Christ and what God's will is for my life. You must recognize that it is a trick of the enemy to keep you uninterested in God's word. If you read God's word, it will begin to challenge the way you think, and that's what Satan fears the most.

Due to the fact that many people are not mentally prepared for what God wants to do in their lives, they must understand that being "transformed by the renewing of your mind" is one of the most important steps in receiving your purpose. Change the way you think and you'll change your life; change what you listen to and entertain and you'll change the way you think. *Junk in, junk out!* If you feed your mind the word of God on a daily basis, you'll develop a mentality based on the word of God. If you feed your mind porn, vulgar lyrics from secular songs, gossip, violent imagery from movies and video games, and negativity from negative people all day, that's what you'll become. The Bible says in Galatians chapter 6 that whatever you sow, that's what you will reap. If you continually sow to the flesh, you'll reap destruction; but if you invest time in God, fellowshipping with the Holy Spirit and reading God's word, then Paul says you will reap life everlasting. It's up to you. If you have a spirit of fear, turn off the television and radio and play the Bible on CD. Play biblical teaching tapes. Invest your time in the things of God and you will find yourself changing gradually. So many of us want someone to lay hands on us and cause all of our habits and strongholds to just fall off of us, but that's not the way it works. You must change your way of thinking, and that takes a dedication and commitment to seeking after knowledge and revelation from God's word.

The source of purpose is God. From him comes life, abundant life. He opens doors no man can open, and closes doors no man can close. But it's about following his plan and walking in his timing. It's about renewing our minds with his word. It's about giving up our pursuits and making his priorities our priorities. It's about taking up our cross. Now is the time to surrender all to God and abandon any idols that may be preventing you from pursuing after Christ with all your heart. If you're ready to do so, I want you to pray the prayer below and also follow the exercise I have for you below.

EXERCISE:

Just like our earlier exercise—in which you made a list of the idols in your life—I want you to make another list in your Purpose Seekers journal in the corresponding section, which is titled "Sins and Weights". This time, I want you to list the sins and weights you may have in your life that are hindrances to you fully accepting God's will. If listening to ungodly music is one of your weights, list it. If watching certain television programming is your weight, list it (porn, horror movies; things that are very demonic in nature). If gossip is your sin, list it. If going to places (atmospheres) that are demonically charged is your weight (certain

---

types of clubs, strip clubs, places that promote lust and perversion, etc.), list it. If watching too much television (whether it be sports, sitcoms, etc.) has become a weight in the fact that it prevents you from devoting time to God, list it. Whatever competes with God in your life, list it. While saying the prayer below, when you come to the parentheses with the blank space in it, I want you to confess one by one each sin and weight that you wrote on your list. Don't worry about how long it takes. This is the act of you declaring deliverance over your life. We're going to denounce the works of the enemy today and declare you to be a new creation who is walking in the newness of Christ Jesus.

PRAY THIS PRAYER:

Heavenly Father, I thank you for your blessings. I thank you for your love. I thank you for saving my soul. Father, I come to you today with a broken and contrite heart. I repent to you for holding onto sins and weights you told me to let go of. Today, I let go of (**state each sin and weight**) today. I denounce these things and choose to live according to your will. I am no longer bound to these sins and weights. I am free in Christ Jesus. As your word says, if any man be in Christ, he/she is a new creation. Old things have already passed away, and all things are made new. I have a changed mind. I have a new spirit. I am a new person, right now. Give me the mind of Christ, which you promised to your people in 2 Corinthians chapter 2. Lord, as I read your word, open my spiritual eyes that I may see your revelation and understand your word. Give me understanding, wisdom and knowledge today. Renew my thinking. For, today, I consecrate my mind, heart and soul to you. My plans, I surrender to you. Let my motives no longer be geared towards pleasing and glorifying my flesh, but doing your will. Give me the right motives for serving you. Give me my cross, my assignment, my task. Let me be focused on winning the lost, and equip me for the task. I thank you. In Jesus name, Amen.

PURPOSE SEEKERS

CHAPTER 3:
HIDDEN TREASURES

RAPUNZEL! RAPUNZEL! LET DOWN YOUR HAIR! That was a line from a movie I saw once: *Tangled.* Although this movie wasn't a Christian based film, it made me think about some things Christians go through. This movie, being a modern twist on a classic tale, was about a young princess named Rapunzel. She had very, very long hair; hair that was magical: whenever she'd sing, her hair would glow; and while glowing, it would heal anyone and anything it touched; it could even reverse the effects of aging. When Rapunzel was just a baby, an old woman named Gothel stole her from her crib and carried her off to a secret location: a tower well hidden in the forest. The only way into and out of the tower was through the entrance that rested at the top of the tower some 20-30 feet high. There was a secret entrance into the tower which didn't become known to Rapunzel until the end of the movie; but until then, Rapunzel knew of only one way into and out of the tower.

Mother Gothel, as she's called in the story, when she would arrive home at the tower, would call out to Rapunzel to let down her hair so she could climb onto it; and while holding onto it, Rapunzel would pull her up to the entrance of the tower. Mother Gothel would periodically comb Rapunzel's hair; and while combing it, she would ask Rapunzel to sing for her. That hair would light up while Mother Gothel was holding it, thereby reversing the effects of aging each time. What Rapunzel didn't know was Mother Gothel was well over a hundred years old, although she appeared to be only in her mid thirties thanks to the magical effects of Rapunzel's hair. Also, Rapunzel didn't know that Mother Gothel wasn't really her mother—that she had actually been kidnapped as a baby by Mother Gothel. For years she affectionately referred to her kidnapper as mother, and saw herself as just an ordinary girl with extraordinary hair. She had no way of knowing she was actually royalty, that she was really the long lost princess. Every year, around her birthday, she'd see floating lanterns ascending into the sky from where the palace was, but she never knew those lanterns were for her—they were being released by everyone in the kingdom as a memorial to her, the long lost princess. Rapunzel felt especially drawn to the lights, but she didn't know why. She knew there was more to her life than sitting in a tower, playing with a pet lizard, and that those lighted lanterns held a deeper meaning than what had been interpreted to her by Mother Gothel. She was eighteen now and was beginning to sense that something wasn't quite right.

This Disney animated tale speaks so much truth today. It reveals the condition of so many of us. Many people today are trapped in towers of isolation, allowing their gifts to be used up by parasitic people who mean them no good, by manipulators who keep them on a tight leash using lies. It is necessary that, along the journey to God's purpose for your life, you learn to identify and avoid parasitic people and exit towers you find yourself languishing in. For they can drain you and zap away your zest, your zeal, your dreams; they can crush the very dreams God has placed inside of you, making you believe that where you are is where you'll always be. We often call these people "dream killers". They're real, and they are out there, lurking in the shadows, waiting to kidnap your potential. And they usually strike when you're very young.

I noticed how in the Bible, anytime Satan wanted to destroy a mighty move of God, he would target the babies for annihilation first. When Moses was born, Pharaoh sent out a decree ordering the execution of all newborn male babies in the land. When Jesus was born, Herod sent out orders to his soldiers to kill all of the newborn male babies in his country. The devil hates babies because they're God-sent; he hates children because of what they can become, because of what they carry inside of them: the potential to change the world for the glory of God. Satan has two goals: corrupt the children so that they'll use their gifts and talents for his will, or kill them so that they can't use their gifts and talents for God's glory.

Here is where I want to plug in a reminder to parents that what they're experiencing with their children is spiritual warfare. Satan wants to snag them early through television programming and music that's of a demonic nature. I remember when my husband stopped our kids from looking at certain cartoon shows. He explained to them that these shows were promoting things that clearly God frowns upon in the Bible. The devil always disguises his message in kid-friendly forms like cartoons. As parents we must guard our children from satanic attacks by grounding them in the word of God early; we must keep them from demonic influences that promote fornication, drugs, and other sinful practices. There are good Christian movies and cartoons (like *Veggie Tales*) your kids can look at. There are TV stations like TBN which have networks like *Smile of a Child*, designed specifically for kids. Now I'm not saying you have to look at TBN all day. My family stays at the movies. We love action flicks, comedies, adventure movies, fantasies, and others; but we also know when something is blatantly demonic. I'm not saying you have to listen to gospel music all day either, but some songs you know are blatantly demonic. But I found this to be the biggest case: if the parents don't honor God, they won't train their children to honor God. If parents are playing nasty and vulgar music, their children will also idolize and embrace nasty and vulgar music, and thereby develop a mentality based on the stuff they hear. That is why Satan wants not only the children under his wings, but their parents: the parents are the biggest influences in a child's life. Non-praying parents won't be powerful enough and discerning enough to shield their children from demonic attacks. Almost nightly, while my mind was under the influence of the enemy, my grandmother in South Carolina had to pray over me in the midnight hour, speaking in tongues over me and casting off spirits that would attack me. If you're a praying parent, I want to encourage you to keep praying for your child. If God could change me, he can change anyone. Like I said earlier in this book: I am the product of someone else's prayers. If my grandmother had not taken the time to intercede on my behalf, I might still be lost today—or dead.

IN THE TOWER

In the movie (*Tangled*), the tower represented isolation. It was hidden deep within the woods. You had to find a secret path just to find it. Isolation is the state of being separated from everyone else. This is how Satan wants God's people: separate from one another. The devil doesn't want Christians to congregate. That is why he tries so hard to keep them from the church: the church is where they get strengthened, refueled, and are often reminded of who they are and what they are supposed to be doing. In church you may hear a word that will lift your spirit, or encounter someone who will pray off satanic bondages. In church God may just send some-one to you with a word, or even a physical blessing (a car, money, a house, job, etc.). And just by sitting at home you could have missed that blessing. God wants his saints to touch and agree, not catch service on tele-vision or the Internet. There's is nothing wrong with watching church on TV or online, but God told us in Hebrews 10:25 to "forsake not the assembling together of the saints," which means get up and go to the house of God. When a sheep wonders away from the flock, it becomes the prime target of the wolves lurking near by. God gave us shepherds (pastors) to stand guard and watch over our souls (Hebrews 13:17).

Like Rapunzel, there are many today who are locked inside of towers of isolation due to the spirit of fear. Mother Gothel was able to maintain a tight grip on Rapunzel simply by convincing her that she wouldn't be able to survive outside of the tower; that the forest around her was populated by monsters and evil men who would take advantage of her. Rapunzel was convinced that she was safe in the tower. That is what the spirit of fear does: convince us that stepping outside of our comfort zones equates to certain death; that if we venture out of our little shells we will get devoured. Satan specializes in keeping us locked in the tower by causing us to constantly imagine every potential danger and disaster. Worry is mainly the process of entertaining disastrous images in our heads. Worry is like a rocking chair: it keeps you moving, but you aren't going anywhere. Jesus asked in Luke chapter 12, who can, by worrying, add an inch on to their lives? If by worrying we can't change our circumstances, then the reasonable thing to do would be to seek for a solution instead of wasting time with worry. Jesus, in that same passage, also told us that the key to overcoming our circumstances is to "seek first the kingdom of God," which means to shift our focus from our problems to developing a closer walk with God and hearing his voice; after all, he has all of the solutions. It's easy to find yourself being ruled by images in your head that were placed there by the enemy. The reality is: in most cases, the things we imagine never even come to pass. But due to worry, we do several things: (1) We do the devil's job for him and torment ourselves. Worry is the complete opposite of faith. It is the act of not trusting God with our situations. It is the act of declaring our own selves God over our circumstances. (2) We make hasty decisions or neglect to make important decisions. (3) We destroy our temples (bodies). Excessive worrying doesn't just affect your mental health, it also wreaks havoc on your physical well-being. One interesting report states, "Worriers are more likely to have irritable bowel syndrome, nausea, fatigue, and aches and pains. In addition, 93% of people with generalized anxiety disorder also have an overlapping psychiatric disorder such as depression" ("9 Steps to end Chronic Worrying"; www.webmd.com).

I can remember a time when I began to be a chronic worrier. I worried about everything: if I was a good mother to my kids, a good wife, a good person, my grades in school; I worried about job interviews and approaching deadlines; I worried about bills, expenses, rising gas prices, insurance costs; I even worried about having my home in perfect condition for company—although it only took a few seconds after their arrival for the house to be turned upside down again. Worrying led to me developing acid reflux. It began to not only be a habit, but a spiritual bondage. The only way I defeated the spirit of worry was by getting back to the word. One thing I noticed was: while worrying more, I tended to spend less time in God's word. I got back to the word of God and was lifted when I read Matthew 6:25 where Jesus told us to stop being "anxious about your life, what you will eat or what you will drink, nor about your body, what you will put on. Is not life more than food and the body more than clothing?" And in verse 32, Jesus reassured us, his children, that God already knows that we need these things. Jesus then gave us the solution to worry when he told us to place our focus on pursuing him rather than thinking about the problem. Also, in Philippians 4:6, 7, Paul reminds us to not be anxious for anything, but pray about everything. Jesus mentioned in Matthew 6:27 that worrying can't add a single moment onto your life; therefore, worrying is unproductive and useless; it's counterproductive because it replaces the time we could be spending receiving solutions from God through prayer. I then began attacking the spirit of worry. In 2 Corinthians 10:4, Paul instructs us to cast down every "thought" and "imagination" (image) that exalts itself against the word of God. The only way to combat the visions, thoughts and dreams planted into your mind by the enemy—visions and dreams sent to torment you and produce fear inside of you (1 John 4:18)—is to attack them with God's word. You must speak the word daily. Declare God's promises over your life. The word is our weapon against the enemy.

Another thing that keeps men in the tower is the fear of failure. Many people will give-up on their goals after one failed attempt. If everyone who failed at a goal gave-up, then Abraham Lincoln would have given up trying to be the President of the United States of America after the first failure. Many great people would've cast their potential aside and settled for the *tower of mediocrity*. Just because you failed once doesn't mean you're a failure. Mike Tyson failed to secure a spot on the Olympic boxing team, but he didn't stop fighting. He even went on to become one of the greatest heavyweight fighters in boxing history. The same is said about Michael Jordan: although he failed to make the varsity basketball team in high school, that failure didn't stop him from playing basketball. In fact, he went on to be one of the greatest basketball players in the history of the sport. If you view yourself as a failure because of a failed attempt, you are robbing yourself of the one thing all successful people had to experience: failures show us the areas we need to strengthen and develop in more. If you never make mistakes, you will never learn what to do right. You grow from mistakes. Many are scared to try because they don't want to fail, but there is no other way to grow. Satan, however, will discourage you from stepping out on faith by frightening you with the possibility of failure. But you must always remember: When God promises you something, it will happen. Whatever dream God gives you will come to pass. He doesn't need your expertise, he simply needs your compliance. A plan you come up with is a maybe, but a plan God devises is a guarantee. So, when God speaks a word to you, you can rest confidently, knowing that you are in the right place, and that you are not gambling with your life. You can then do as Rapunzel did and let your feet touch the grass below. Just don't let Mother Gothel send you scaling back up the tower wall.

EXPOSING AND DEFEATING MOTHER GOTHEL

Some people are sent by God into our lives, and some people are sent by Satan. Jesus said in Matthew chapter 13 that not every person is sent by God to us. Some people are tares, not wheat. Tares are weeds which choke the life out of the wheat, killing it slowly. In the story,

Mother Gothel kept Rapunzel around only so that she could use her gift. She cared nothing for Rapunzel as a person. You may have people around you that are only there because you have a gift that can benefit them; they aren't concerned about you, just what you can do for them. God sends people into your life to pour into you, not drain you. God sends you to people to pour into them, not use and drain them. Every gift God gives... gives. Satan, on the other hand, drains us through selfish people who only demand, demand, demand but never pray for us, encourage us, support us, help us remain accountable to God, partner with us, and roll-up their sleeves when they're needed. Some people zap your energy through words of discouragement every time you attempt to step out on faith. They remind you of how impossible it is to do what God is telling you to do, forgetting that you can "do all things through Christ, which strengtheneth us" (Philippians 4:13), and that "all things are possible to them which believe" in God (Mark 9:23). They bring up your mistakes rather than talk about your accomplishments. They love to remind you of where you came from rather than talk about where you're going. They appreciate your gift, but fear your vision. They don't want you to get a vision from God for your life. If you receive a vision from God, you'll stop living out their vision. Mother Gothel only benefits from your spiritual blindness, your lack of faith and a prayer life, your fear of stepping out on faith, and your feeling of discouragement. Sadly, Mother Gothel sees in you something you don't see in yourself. She knows you have a gift that is extraordinary. She recognizes your potential. This is why she fights all the more to keep you grounded in fear and insecurity, and to prevent you from seeing yourself the way God sees you. But if you're going to overcome Mother Gothel, you must see yourself the way God does. In 2 Corinthians 5:16, Paul tells us to "know no man after the flesh". He urged us instead to view ourselves and others through a spiritual lens. Don't look at where they are; look at where God desires to take them. Don't look at what they're doing; look at what they could be doing for the kingdom of God. Don't look at what's going on with them physically; look at what's going on with them spiritually. The same is to be said regarding you. Stop looking at where you are, and look at the place God is trying to send you to. He has greatness in store for all of his people. We are the "workmanship" of his hands created for "every good work" (Ephesians 2:10). Recognize that Mother Gothel is a victim too—a victim of deception. So don't get mad at her, become bitter, hateful, vengeful, or walk in un-forgiveness; simply pray for her deliverance while walking forward into your bright future.

If there's one thing Mother Gothel did well, it is this: she kept Rapunzel on a leash by keeping her feeling guilty about leaving the tower. Mother Gothel pretended to be a nurturing, caring individual; she pretended to be a protector. Mother Gothel would occasionally appease Rapunzel by bringing back gifts. She knew that if Rapunzel would lower her expectations, she'd be satisfied with small things. If Rapunzel would have remained in that tower and not discovered that she was the princess, she would have kept a low opinion of herself and remained grateful for scraps when she was actually destined to sit at the king's table. Are you thankful for scraps, or has it sunk in yet that as a child of God you are supposed to be seated at the King's table? Are you simply glad to just get by—to get just enough to pay the rent this month, to get just enough to pay the bills this month, to get just enough to get a hamburger off of the dollar menu this time? Or have you recognized that we who're Christians are "seated in heavenly places" with God, and that God's desire is to do "exceeding abundantly above all that we ask or think" (Ephesians 3:20)? I'm sure you can imagine more than just having a light bill paid. But Mother Gothels come to keep your expectations low so that you'll remain grateful for sub-standard blessings. You have a right—I'm sorry, let me rephrase that: You have an obligation to hold high standards. If you're starting out small, expect to finish big. Don't look forward to remaining where you are. If God promised you a mate, expect someone who's going to treat you like a queen, or a king, not someone who's going to abuse you and treat you like dirt. No one is perfect, but a true Christian has standards and demands respect; they also treat others with respect, and walk in the love of God towards others. As Paul explained in Romans chapter 13 and 1 Corinthians chapter 13, love does not seek to hurt, abuse, misuse, destroy, manipulate, discourage, kill, steal, lie on, exploit, and lead anyone into sin. These are standards you should have and demand out of those around you. When I was younger, boys would touch me in the wrong places and I would assume that it was alright because it was the norm in my environment. It wasn't until I got older that I discovered that what they were doing was violating my body, and that I had allowed them to get away with treating me like dirt. I didn't know that I deserved respect as a young lady...and that I was supposed to demand respect out of those around me. God wants the best for us as his children. He wants you healed, delivered, blessed, happy, content, in a state of peace, and resting confidently in him. He does not want you acting like a mindless slave. He even calls us "friends" in John 15:15. His desire is to develop an intimate relationship with us, not treat us like servants. He wants intimacy with you, not acts of service from you. There is nothing you can do to impress God. All you can do is sit at his feet and allow him to press, mold and shape you into the person he wants you to be. He gets pleasure out of molding and shaping us, and blessing us. But if you allow the Mother Gothels in your life to continue to manipulate you, they will keep you feeling guilty about desiring greater for yourself. It is God's will that you desire greater; that you look out of the window and be magnetically drawn to the lights floating in the distance. There is a divine agitation in your spirit pulling you to another level, telling you that there is more to your life than what you're currently experiencing. This agitation is letting you know that God has more for you, and that you don't belong where you are. You're an eagle living in the hen house. You're a king, a queen, living like a peasant. You're the Father's son living in a pig-pen, eating the pig's slop despite having a seat designated for you at the Father's table. Expect more and release that demonic yoke of guilt. It's natural to feel guilty over sin (1 John 3:19-22), but it's not natural to feel guilty over wanting to do more to serve God's kingdom.

In Hebrews chapters 9 and 10, the writer talks

about being free from the "conscience" of sin and "dead works". What he was referring to were the many ceremonial practices outlined in the Old Testament law (things like the Temple sacrifices, showing yourself to a priest if you had a boil on your skin, etc.). He was not referring to God's moral precepts such as those found in the 10 Commandments. What the writer was really saying was: as Christians under a better covenant with God through Christ Jesus, we should no longer feel guilty for not being able to keep up with all of those old ceremonial practices. Don't feel guilty over things God never commanded you to do, or things God has done away with. If you're feeling guilty over something today, ask yourself if what you're feeling guilty over is something God instructed you to do or something God didn't instruct you to do. That makes all of the difference. Some children feel guilty over disobeying things their parents told them to do, but the issue is this: Is what your parents telling you to do in line with God's will, or does it oppose God's will. For example, if your parents instruct you to lie on their behalf, or steal, or even hate (many parents teach their children to be racists) and kill, then you will have to choose between obeying your parents or obeying God who tells us not to steal, kill, hate, and lie in his word. Remembeer: It's *your soul* on the line. Jesus said in Matthew 10:37, if we love our parents or children more than him, we're not worthy of him—that means no one comes before God and instruct us to do that which God forbids in his word. You should never feel guilty over disobeying any instruction that opposes God's moral commandments; actually, you should feel proud that you stood up for Christ...despite who didn't like it. In the Bible God's people were demonized, criminalized, and persecuted because they stood for God in defiance of corrupt governmental leaders and their unjust laws that promoted sin; but because of their stance, they were rewarded by God in heaven. If you conform your thinking to the word of God, you will find yourself feeling less and less guilty over things people have long held you accountable to. You'll realize these things (obligations, traditions, expectations) were never God's design for you to begin with; and at that moment, you'll stop feeling bad because you decided to leave *the tower*.

EXERCISE:

Before we move on, I want you to take a moment and reflect on your current circumstance. I want you to consider where you are. Are you in a tower of isolation; and if so, who or what drove you to that place? What thoughts have the enemy been placing in your mind to keep you isolated? Has he been ruling your life with the fear of rejection, the fear of failure, the fear of lost and pain? I want you to write down the things God has instructed you to do and the promises he has declared over your life in your journal, and list the things the enemy has been using to stop you from pursuing what God called you to. I also want you to reflect on the people in your life, both past and present, who have been influential in your life. Examine whether or not they have been a godly influence or a destructive one. If they've been a destructive influence, I want you to write their names down on

---

your list, as well as all of the hurtful and destructive words they have spoken to you (as much as you can remember). After you've listed their names and their words, we're going to make a few declarative statements at the end of this chapter over them and over our own lives. Don't worry: everything we're going to declare is for the purpose of blessing, not cursing anyone. In our prayer at the end of this chapter, I want you to state the negative and destructive words that have been spoken over your life in the blank space asking for those statements. Also, when you come to the blank space asking for you to state the names of those who negatively impacted your life, I want you to state their names.

FLOATING LANTERNS

God will guide us using our own spirits. The Bible says the deep calls out to the deep (1 Corinthians 2:10-11). The Holy Spirit, according to Paul in 1 Corinthians 2:12, has a way of placing desires in our hearts during our fellowship with him. He begins to show us things that are "freely given" unto us by God, things no one else is designed to have but us. In Philippians 2:13, Paul said God will both give us the desire to do his will and work within us to accomplish it. But he mentioned our desires first. God first changes our desires, then changes our direction in life. All of this comes only through prayer and fellowship with the Holy Spirit. Without first yielding to the Holy Spirit, our desires will be in the wrong place. And quite naturally, the flesh, as stated in Proverbs 16:2, always thinks it is right. Until God steps in and removes the spiritual scales from our eyes, we'll always think we're on the right track.

I remember when God first dealt with me concerning my husband. He had been prophesied to that he would find a wife at an early age, one that would be beautiful—I mean, I'm not bad looking—and would help him in ministry. The prophet told him, "You will know her when you see her." This was in 1998. The next year, Timothy (my husband) began mentoring my brother. We had never met before. I didn't know him, and he didn't know me. I had seen him in teens ministry, but really didn't feel any type of connection to him. But as I kept drawing close to God, suddenly I began to notice things about him that I hadn't noticed before. I began to develop an attraction to him. To make a long story short (and save the rest for another book), God set us up on a blind date. One day, several friends and I (around 15 people, including Timothy) were planning to go to the skating ring, but then it ended up being only me and Timothy after everyone else backed out at the last minute. I was attracted to him, and he confessed he was secretly attracted to me. Before that, God set us up to be around each other after, of all things, we were assigned to escort one another during a wedding scene in a fashion show we both participated in—at the time of the fashion show we hardly knew each other, but had to mock-marry each other in that scene. Even then God was orchestrating events. Years later when Timothy proposed to me, he stated that he'd already known I was to be his wife. Nothing was forced. God set everything up in his own way. But he started with our desires—with me noticing things and even looking for things I would have never noticed in a mate or looked for in a mate had I not found Christ first, and Timothy learning to look for specific qualities in a mate after God changed his heart and mind. My husband told me that the revelation he got out of the prophesy given to him was that by "You will know her when you see her," that meant he would grow spiritually so that he would recognize what he needed in order to complete the mission God had for him. It's not that a halo would float over his future wife's head, but that he'd discover his purpose; and hence, discover who's best suited to walk beside him in it. He told me about the process he underwent to mature to the level of knowing what to look for: how he had to allow God to take him on a journey internally to discover who he was and what he needed to be delivered from. He was led to a Christian bookstore where God placed him on a quest of self discovery. Along the journey, he discovered he was praying for the wrong things. God had to change his desires so that he'd start asking for the right things. He testified that after God finished dealing with him, he stopped asking God to send him someone that would satisfy his need for companionship, and changed his prayer to "God send me to someone I can bless and help fulfill your purpose in." The moment he stopped focusing on himself and started focusing on being a vessel of God's used to bless others, God brought us together.

As you draw close to God, he will begin to transform your desires. He will cause you to notice things about yourself and others you didn't notice before. It's not that others need to change around you; but sometimes, you are the one that needs to change. You may be walking through life with expectations that have nothing to do with God's will for you, and that is why you are unfulfilled—you are chasing after things and trying to accomplish goals that weren't even designed for you. You can succeed at accomplishing the wrong goals. But as you draw close to God, you'll begin to notice just how far off base you've been and just how far away from your place of destiny you really are. You'll see the lanterns in the distance and will start to feel the sudden need to leave the place where you are mentally, spiritually, and maybe even physically.

God, in Romans 11:14, said he blessed the gentile Believers so that he could make the Jews jealous. When noticing the joy, peace, contentment, and clarity of direction God's people have, it should actually make you envious...enough to desire the type of closeness to God that they have. Don't covet their material possessions; envy their walk with God. Yes, be envious of their walk, so much so that you run to the altar and say, "God I want to know you more. I want that type of peace and joy." Paul said in 1 Corinthians 12:31, we should "covet earnestly the best gifts". And there's no greater gift than the Holy Spirit (Luke 11:11-13).

The floating lanterns represent the spiritual blessings of God. Too many people are already distracted by the "lust of the flesh" (1 John 2:16). They're looking at...floating cars, houses, careers, etc. But what they should be looking at are the floating lanterns of God's peace, joy, favor, and intimacy with him. The lanterns came from the location of the palace in...the kingdom. They were a sign to Rapunzel that she'd been taken from her rightful place in the kingdom. God is trying to draw us to...the kingdom of God. The kingdom of God is not religion; it's a fulfilling relationship with the Holy Spirit leading to an abundance of joy, peace and power in our souls (Romans 14:17). When we discover who we are—that we belong in the kingdom—and get back to our rightful places in Christ, we'll recognize our uniqueness and walk in it.

In 2 Corinthians 4:7, Paul said God has placed great treasure in our "earthen vessels". This treasure refers to your purpose, your passion, and your gifts. There are some dreams God has placed deep, deep inside of you that you don't even know are there; and only until you get connected with him will you discover the treasure already buried inside of you. If you need money, God has already placed something inside of you that can bring great wealth into your possession. There's no need to run to and fro to find an idea. God has given you his Spirit, and his Spirit has all of the ideas. Deuteronomy 29:29 says, "The secret things belong to God." God wants to share with you life-changing, wealth-generating, earth-shaking secrets. He only shares them with those he trusts, those close to him, those who love him enough to give up the world for him.

You can't find the treasure of God inside you without the assistance of the Holy Spirit. Proverbs 20:27 says that our spirits are the candlestick of the Lord, used by him to search out our innermost parts. The Holy Spirit uses our spirits like lamps when searching our hearts. Only he is able to do so. We, on the other hand, don't possess the ability to know what's truly in our hearts. Jeremiah 17:9 tells us, "The human heart is the most deceitful of all things, and desperately wicked.

Who really knows how bad it is?" (NLT). But in the 10th verse, God says, "But I, the Lord, search all hearts and examine secret motives..." We must rely on God's Spirit to tell us what's inside of us. When we look within rather than look to God, we are taking matters into our own hands and attempting to do what only God can do. We are trusting in our flesh rather than relying on God. Philippians 3:3 tells us to put "no confidence" in ourselves; but rather, place all of our confidence in God. We can't save and deliver ourselves, neither can we lead our own lives. The only thing we can do is to continually present our hearts to the Holy Spirit and ask him to search them, mold and shape them, place within them the right desires, take out of them the wrong desires, and bring to the forefront the treasures buried deep inside of them.

FLYNN RIDER

In the movie *Tangled*, Rapunzel was fortunate enough to come into contact with a thief named Flynn Rider. He was on the run from the authorities at the time, and had found the tower where Rapunzel was hiding. He scaled the side of the tower wall and snuck into the tower. He didn't expect to find a beautiful young girl there, but he did. He found the princess without knowing it. In the movie, Flynn was more than a young handsome, charming thief; he became a guide to Rapunzel. He encouraged her to step out of the tower and let her feet touch the green grass below. God sent his Spirit to be your Flynn Rider: a guide who's here to help you venture out of your tower and step into your destiny. You can't make it without a Flynn Rider. God uses people in our lives to be a Flynn Rider in our lives. They encourage us to leave our places of complacency and fear and to take a leap of faith into the things God has called us to. God not only calls us, but he sends help our way to aid us as we walk out his will for our lives. Be on the look out for help; God is sending it. It may already be there. There is always someone the Holy Spirit is using to guide us. All we have to do is be willing to receive guidance.

PRAY THIS PRAYER:

Dear heavenly Father, thank you for your many wonderful blessings. I thank you that I am your child, and that you have accepted me into your kingdom. I acknowledge that I am a citizen of your kingdom. I am your child. I am not an ordinary individual. I am uniquely made. I am the workmanship of your hands, created for every good work. I was fearfully and wonderfully made by you. Today, I denounce the world and the works of Satan. I cast down every thought and imagination in my mind that exalts itself against your word. I take authority over thoughts of fear, of worry, and of tragedy and failure. I thank you that no weapon formed against me and my family shall prosper. I cast down every nightmare and every image sown in my mind by the enemy. I acknowledge that everything the devils says is a lie. I also thank you that all things are working out for my good because I love you.

Today, Father, I exercise my kingdom authority and speak against every word curse spoken over

---

my life from my childhood up. I know that the enemy sent agents to speak death into my future, to speak defeat, failure, and lack; but I declare that every condemning and destructive declaration and decree that has been made over my life is now null and void. I replace every word curse with the promise of God. I thank you that whereas it was spoken over my life that I am and would always be (**state the negative words on your list**), your word declares differently. I am not the things that were declared over me. I am more than a conquerer through Christ Jesus. I am the head and not the tail, above and not beneath, blessed and highly favored, prosperous, wealthy, free from generational curses and bondages, strong and mighty in God; I am a person of godly character, of godly standards, one deserving of the best because of who I serve.

I also thank you, heavenly Father, for everyone I've ever crossed paths with. I thank you even for those who spoke negatively into my life. Although they were used by the enemy to discourage and destroy me, what the devil meant for evil you turned around for my good. I pray for (**state the names of the people on your list**). Father, I pray for their healing and deliverance. I forgive them. I choose to walk in love towards them. I believe you for their salvation if they do not know you in the pardon of their sins. And I pray that you will open their eyes so that they may see your will for their lives, just as you have opened mine.

Lastly, I thank you Holy Spirit for giving me the right desires so that I will desire God's perfect plan for my life. Search my heart Holy Spirit. I give you complete and total permission to do whatever you want to do with me and through me. Cleanse my heart. Give me a clean heart and a right spirit. Reveal to me what treasures you have placed inside of me. Let me not bury these treasures and not use them for your glory. I will not walk in fear. I will not succomb to the spirit of fear. I will not fear increace, prosperity, acquiring new skills, reaching new heights, encountering new people; I will not fear rejection, opportunities, changes, and challenges. I have been given your Spirit so that I may walk in love, peace, assurance and divine confidence. For I do not place any trust and confidence in my flesh and my ability, but I place all of my trust and confidence in you, and depend upon you wholeheartedly to lead me. This I ask, in Jesus name, Amen.

CHAPTER 4:
DIVORCING DARKNESS

S OME PEOPLE HATE TO HEAR THE WORD "NO." It is as if that word is a dagger plunged deep into their hearts; or better yet, their egos. For some people, the word "no" is an insult to their pride. Either they have never been told *no* before, or they have been made to believe that they should always get what they want. Some people have an entitlement mentality which makes them think the world is theirs. They didn't create this world, and they didn't create anything in it; but they believe they own the title deeds to everything therein simply because...they exist.

It is an extremely dangerous thing to think the world revolves around you. Such an attitude will only cause you to disrespect others. It will cause you to disregard the rights and personal space of others, it will also cause you to assume that everyone else is supposed to think and feel the way you do. Even Paul, in Romans

14:1-5, stressed that Believers aren't to force their views on anyone, but rather give people the freedom to be convinced in their own minds of the truth. Tell them the truth, but leave it to the Holy Spirit to bring the conviction and do the converting. But if you're a selfish person, you think differently. If someone were to disagree and differ with you, they would be in danger of facing your wrath. If they don't do what you want them to do, they will be in danger of your wrath. If you decide to leave a selfish person, they might threaten you with destruction and even death. This is demonstrated in so many relationships where one person is controlling and abusive. The abusive one doesn't want anyone to disagree with them or disobey their wishes. They really want people to bow down and kiss their feet. They really have an addiction. You see, selfishness never gets tired of being catered to. A person who craves power and control can never have enough power and control. The more they get, the more they crave. The more you bow down to a bully, the more they bully you...because the more you cower in the face of selfishness, the bigger it grows. My oldest son loves to look at The Incredible Hulk. Whenever Bruce Banner gets angry, he turns into a big green monster. The angrier Hulk gets, the bigger he grows. That's the same thing that happens to selfishness: the more you give in to it, the bigger and more controlling it grows. The only way to stop this big green monster is to stand up to it and declare enough is enough. Leave that house if that man keeps beating on you. The longer you stay there, the more he'll do it. When he sees that you have standards and that you won't take that crap anymore he will either straighten up or move on. Let that bully know that you aren't going to take their crap anymore. Stand up to evil. Stand up to that habit, and that addiction that keeps pushing you around. Tell it enough is enough. Whatever you allow to continue to run rampant in your life will continue to run rampant. You have the power to change some things. Even sinners change everyday without the help of God: they break addictions, change habits and lifestyles, obtain success in their endeavors, etc. So just imagine what you can do with the help of God. That's why Paul said in Romans chapter 6 we must stop allowing sin to rule in our bodies (meaning our lives). He also said the more you yield to sin, the more dominion it will have over you. You can either empower that bully, abusive spouse, spoiled child, addiction or sin, or you can put an end to their reign of terror by deciding the buck stops here.

Sometimes God has to wait until we grow tired of some things before he moves in our lives. Many people are still enjoying their bondages and sins; therefore, they are not ready to be delivered. Jesus met a Samaritan woman at a well and confronted her about her promiscuous lifestyle so that she would stop jumping from man to man and let God work in her life. Jesus met a woman caught in the act of adultery and told her to "go and sin no more." She had to get tired of living the way she did before God could do anything else in her life. Jesus, after healing a blind man, told him to "stop sinning or something worst will come upon you." Each of us has the power to turn our backs on the world, but we have to grow tired of the world before we can change.

In James chapter 4, the writer refers to Christians who still love and seek to befriend the world as "adulterers and adulteresses". An adulterer is someone who cheats on their spouse. God said that by loving the world we're really cheating on him. No one trusts a cheater. No one! And if trust is a determining factor as to whether God will bless us or not, then being a cheater doesn't help much. God even condemned the priests in Malachi chapter 2 because of their unfaithfulness to their wives. He said he would ignore their prayers if they continued to be unfaithful and abusive to the wives of their youth. God takes covenant very seriously, including and especially the marriage covenant. Marriage is an institution that can only be upheld by mature individuals who know what they want, people who're tired of games and nonsense. They know the grass on the other side might look green, but it's still just grass—and it's artificial. God wants to bless us, but we must grow up first and stop wasting time. In Galatians chapter 4, Paul talked about the Believer who is an heir to the promises, but cannot walk in them because they're still childish. When we grow and mature spiritually, God can trust us with greater things. And as we grow spiritually, we will grow tired of games and agitated by those who do not want to take things seriously. So, sometimes God isn't saying no; he's simply saying, "Not now. You're not ready yet. I need you to grow up."

THE GROWING STAGE

I had finally come to Christ after all of that praying by my grandmother. When I moved back to Atlanta I began going to church with my aunt. I joined the church after being convicted by the word. I then made a complete 180 degree turn in my life. I stopped smoking, stopped fornicating, stop hanging with drug dealers and selling drugs, stopped cursing and acting *hoochie-fied*. This is how big of a change I made practically overnight: I went from being a rebellious teenager who dated drug dealers, lived promiscuously, took and also sold drugs, to being nominated as "Ms. U.G.I." at Banneker High School (U.G.I. stood for Under God's Influence. It was a Christian club that met at our school during after school hours). It's amazing how God can change your life. I went from being called a freak to being called a Jesus girl. I made a change in the way I presented myself. I went from wearing skimpy clothing to wearing suits and summer dresses daily. I didn't want the type of attention from guys that I used to get in the streets anymore. I told my past "goodbye!" The thing that probably had the biggest impact on me during that time in my life was the sermon "No More Sheets" by Prophetess Juanita Bynum. Every word she spoke pierced right through me. She had me crying and repenting, and laying on my face in the den of my aunt's apartment. I had never experienced anything like that before. I got filled with the Holy Spirit while listening to that message that evening. It was the power of the Holy Spirit that radically changed my life. It was an instant change, not a gradual one. I can testify that miracles do happen. I'm one!

I was a freshman in high school when the popular guy took an interest in me. He was a star football player at the school, and all of the girls were after him. He wanted to hook up with me. We started talking, and going out, but he soon broke up with me because he claimed that he never went out with a girl for as long as he did with me without having sex with her. But my mind was made up and I was in love with Jesus. When I'd go to the teens ministry at my church, I felt somewhat out of place because many of the other teens there were acting like what I came out of in the streets: guys were flirting, trying to hook up with girls; the girls were acting promiscuous, some of them; some of the teens there didn't seem as if they were ready and willing to grow in God, and therefore acted uninterested in the word of God as it was being ministered. I really didn't want to be in that type of setting. My mind was focused on growing in God. I was tired of the world, the streets, games and mess, and I didn't have time for it. I noticed a few teens who took God seriously—my now husband being one. When I first saw him, I noticed he always looked serious, as if he was in deep thought. As it later turned out, he took God and the word of God very seriously. If I became a no-nonsense girl, I knew that only a no-nonsense guy would be compatible with me. He had his story, his reasons for longing after God. Both of us had to make sacrifices, and not just once. I gave up the streets for God; and later on, after being sought after by several agencies from New York and Los Angeles after attending IMTA (International Modeling and Talent Association) in Hollywood California in 2002, I made the sacrifice to give it all up just to focus on what I knew God was telling me to do at the time. My husband, in 1995, entered into the ministry, but that was only after he gave up the opportunity to compete for a spot on the Olympic boxing team. Sacrifices must be made, but God always compensates us for these sacrifices later on. When you turn down a dream to follow God's plan, he'll bless you for it (Mark 10:29-30; Hebrews 6:11).

I was completely changed—or so I thought. I was attending every Bible study at the church, singing in the choir, attending prayer services, and was very active in the church as well as a Christian organization at school. I was in the Christian faith sincerely. I was truly growing spiritually. But like any jealous and controlling person who hates being told no, Satan grew angry, jealous, and vengeful. He wanted me back. He wasn't done plotting against me. The devil will always try to get you back after you've left him. Whenever you kick the enemy out of your life, expect him to return. And return he did. The joyride of uninterrupted spiritual growth had suddenly halted, and I found myself now wrestling with a demon from my past I thought I had defeated.

THE OBITUARY

Prior to coming to Christ, while living in sin, I was dating a boy in my old neighborhood. He was the first guy I ever had sex with—at the time I was 12 years old; he was much older than me. I was in-love with him...or so I thought. He was all I thought about. But suddenly, he was gone. He was killed in a motorcycle accident. His untimely death sent me into a state of depression, contemplating suicide. I cried, grieved, played crazy music with the shades drawn, and stayed in the dark.

Let's fast forward. Several years had passed and I had surrendered my life to Christ. The past was behind me...supposedly. But suddenly, during this period of drawing closer to God, I found myself wrestling with a demon I thought I had defeated. I began to have certain dreams. Every night the boyfriend who died would come to me in my dreams and ask me to join him. He'd come to me in different ways. For example, in one dream he came to me driving a car. I got in the car and the two of us were driving along a seemingly endless stretch of road. He was claiming he loved me and that he wanted me to be with him. These nightly visitations grew worse as time progressed. Night after night he'd visit me and ask me to follow him into the darkness—the other side. Some of those old emotions began to resurface. I began thinking I was really supposed to be with him. That's how strong the demonic attack was against me. Things I thought I was completely over took me by surprise. I even began clubbing again and found myself slowly straying from God. I felt as if I had been sucker punched in the spirit. I was caught off guard by a sudden demonic attack. Satan was sitting back waiting for me to get comfortable, to let my guard down and think he was finished attacking me, and then he decided to strike unexpectedly. That is why we must learn spiritual warfare—how to strategize and think like a warrior. We have to understand how wars are fought and won. In 2 Corinthians 2:11, Paul said Christians should never be ignorant of Satan's strategies and methods, lest he gain an advantage over us. When Christians say you shouldn't talk about demonology and witchcraft "lest you give it power over you," they're wrong. Actually, they're not just wrong; they're completely deceived. The less you address Satan's strategies, the more leverage you give him against you. And it was at this point I began to learn about something called "open doors".

After several weeks of experiencing these nightly visitations, I went to the pastor of my church for counseling. I shared with him my past and what was going on in my life at the time. He then explained to me about familiar spirits and open doorways in the spirit. I had experienced spirits in my room when I was younger. I experienced physical attacks by demonic spirits before I got saved. When living in sin, demons easily invade our lives. However, this was the first time I was introduced to the reality that demons can and often do take on the appearances of those who've gone on before us. The reason they're called familiar spirits in the Bible is because they transform themselves to look like that which is familiar to us. In my case, a demonic spirit was now tormenting me nightly, trying to bring up old feelings and get me to backtrack into an old depression. It was trying to lure me back into a suicidal mind. The truth is: unless he repented, that old boyfriend died a sinner. In fact, at his funeral I discovered the other girlfriends he was sleeping with. I had foolishly assumed I was his one and only. I was depressed and suicidal over a guy who not only was sleeping around on me with other girls, but also...other guys. Oh, how we mess ourselves up because we don't know the full story. If I had taken my life after his death, I would have died the ultimate and most selfish fool. I wasn't looking and thinking ahead when younger. Sometimes God has to keep us because we are so shortsighted we make stupid decisions based off of partial information. I didn't see a wonderful husband and three wonderful kids in my future. I didn't see myself being a mighty woman of God, touching lives all around me for the glory of God. I didn't see myself in a better predicament, living a better life than I was living back then. I didn't even know I was just a side chic, a spare tire he'd tell lies to just for some sex...

when he wasn't with his other girlfriends and male sexual partners. I didn't even realize I was on the verge of catching an STD. But, back to my earlier point: unless he surrendered to Christ before taking his final breath, then he died in his sins. His lifestyle was one that was condemned by God. If he didn't repent, then he isn't in heaven; he's in hell. That spirit, disguising itself as my old boyfriend, kept urging me to come to where he was—that meant it wanted me in hell. Hell isn't worth it for anyone. Even if my husband suddenly decides that he wants to go to hell, I still wouldn't follow him...regardless of how much I sincerely love him—it just isn't worth it. In hell, you burn in flames and experience unbearable torments from demons. There are no family reunions, parties, and good times down there. You will be too busy screaming and writhing in agony and pain to even notice who's burning in the pit beside yours. Though surrounded by millions and millions of people, you are always alone down there. There's no love down there since God is love and his presence isn't there. The dumbest thing anyone can do is give up God's wonderful future for them and lose their soul just to follow someone to hell. In heaven there are reunions all the time. You forget about the cares of this life and experience total bliss, joy and indescribable peace and happiness. And the best part about heaven is: this bliss, joy, peace and happiness, reunion with the loved ones who made it in, and ecstasy never wears off and comes to an end; it is never interrupted by spiritual sucker punches. You never have to worry about the storm behind the calm...because storms don't exist up there. It's so wonderful in heaven that Paul, after seeing heaven with his own two eyes (2 Corinthians 12:2-4), longed to be freed from his mortal body. He even debated with himself over whether or not he would choose to die or choose to stay on the earth and help the churches he founded (Philippians 1:23). He longed to go back to heaven so bad that the thought of death actually excited him.

After Pastor Flemming, Sr. finished explaining to me about familiar spirits in our counseling session, while under the anointing, the Holy Spirit prompted him to ask me if I was holding onto any items that represented my old boyfriend. I told him that I still had a copy of his obituary, which I slept with under my pillow every night; also, I kept some of the clothes he bought me. The pastor told me to get rid of all of those items. He told me to trash them, or burn them if I had to; but, whatever the case, those items had to go because they were creating an open door for that familiar spirit to use to enter into my life through. Even as Christians we can give demons access into our lives. It doesn't matter how much you sing, dance, or even pray; if you keep open doors in your home and in your life, demonic spirits will come and go as they please. An open door is anything that is of a demonic nature: this includes certain movies (horror movies, etc.), pornography, drugs and alcohol, sins we won't repent of, and cursed objects such as those found in the occult (Ouija boards, spells and incantations, horoscopes, voodoo objects, etc.). Cursed objects are big open doors. These items can easily be found in your household. Many go undetected. God began dealing with me even regarding the brand of weave I wear due to the fact that some weave is cursed being that it's dedicated to demon spirits (Hindu gods). When you receive the gift of discernment from the Holy Spirit, you begin to become sensitive to certain jewelries and even clothes you wear; you start to feel a demonic presence in certain places, on certain films, and even over inanimate objects (Ezekiel 13:20). At the time, the cursed item I kept in my life was that obituary. That paper wasn't the problem; it was my devotion and emotional attachment to it that gave power to it—that made it an idol in my life. You can make an idol out of anything and anyone, including godly people. If you're not careful, you might find yourself so attached to someone that you create an open doorway through the spirit of grief. Release that loved one and place your focus back on God, lest you end up making them your idol. God wouldn't let the Israelites possess the body of Moses after his death so that they couldn't make an idol out of it. Jesus even told one man that if he was going to follow him he'd have to let "the dead bury the dead." In ancient Israel, the people worshipped idols made out of stone. The stone wasn't the problem; it was their devotion to and reliance upon those stones that was. In the eyes of men, those stones represented gods; therefore, those stone idols became the doorways for demons into the land. You might own something in your home that symbolizes that which is demonic. Get rid of it! It doesn't matter how much it cost you, where you got it from, or how much sentimental value you've placed on it; if it's an artifact that represents idols and idol gods, whether it be an ancient god or the gods currently being worshipped, it's a cursed item that must go. You can't pray, shout, or sing it out; you must toss it out, and then your prayers and worship will not be hindered. God told the Israelites to first get rid of the idols in their land, and then he would honor their prayers once more. God told Joshua to get rid of the man who disobeyed his orders regarding the city of Jericho first, and then he'd give them victory over their enemy (Joshua 7:1-26). Paul, in 2 Corinthians 6:14-18, instructs us to separate from darkness and let go of "unclean" things (cursed objects) first, then God will receive us and be a father to us again. Obedience comes before a sacrifice.

After I got rid of the obituary the dreams ceased; that's because the door the spirit was using to enter into my life had finally been shut. When we shut the door to the enemy, the atmosphere around us will start to clear up, and we'll begin to feel God's presence again.

DROPPING YOUR SECRET LOVERS

My future in God was being put in jeopardy by a secret covenant I had with my past. I thought I was out of the devil's reach because of all of the outer changes I made (to my appearance, surroundings, etc.); but inwardly, I was still married to yesterday because of open doors and soul-ties. My life of promiscuity came with a price. Sin always come with a price. All of those guys I slept with were still affecting me in the form of soulties. The Bible says that whenever two people have sex they become "one flesh". So you can imagine how many people I inwardly married just by living promiscuously. Sometimes we wonder why the enemy still manages to tamper with our spirits when we suppose to belong to God. We automatically assume that our spirits are free from the grip of yesterday the moment we get saved. Yes, your sins may be forgiven automatically, but there's still a process of deliverance that has to take place in the Believer's life, especially if they've opened up too many doorways to the enemy through ignorance as I'd done. Without the knowledge of the word, we perish. Satan prefers that you just jump and shout as opposed to learn the word. He likes you better when you're religious and bound. God began to take me through a process of deliverance by first leading me into a divorcement from the soul-ties I established. I had to openly announce my divorce from these ties. I had to allow God to purge me from all of those ties. It doesn't take God long to deliver a person; it does, however, take long for some people to arrive at the place in their lives where they truly want to be delivered. I had reached that point, knowing that I'd no longer be able to continue to walk in my purpose while still shackled to the past. I had come to the place where I had to let God take some deeply hidden attachments out of my life.

When God is cleansing you, he's preparing you for something great. Some storms come into our lives to show us what is still left inside of us from yesterday. The Bible says we must "lay apart all filthiness and superfluity of naughtiness" in our lives after we get saved (James 1:21). The word "superfluity" means "residue: the wickedness remaining over in a Christian from their state prior to their conversion" in the Greek language. There may be some residue from your life prior to Christ that must be dealt with. Sure, your sins have all been washed away by the blood of Christ; but some open doorways, contracts with spirits, items from your past, old habits, mind-states, and ways are still hindering you. Although saved, you're still in the flesh; and as long as you're in the flesh, you'll have to fight with your own sinful tendencies, habits and ways. The fight doesn't end until the day you die. The more you consecrate yourself unto God, the higher and further he'll take you. Consecrate more and you'll receive more clarity of his purpose. Consecrate more and you'll gain more and more power over the flesh and Satan. Die more to *self* and you will discover more of God, and who you truly are. In John 14:30, Jesus told his disciples that Satan was soon to come, but that Satan would have "nothing in me." Tests will come; but when they come, what will they reveal in you? The Bible says in Ephesians 5:13, everything in the dark will be brought to the light. When the spotlight shines on you, will people discover you have a secret life? Will you have any Word in you to fight the devil with? If all you can say is, "My pastor said..." then you're not ready. You must be able to say like Jesus did, "It is written..." when you're being tested by the devil.

In Matthew 17:21, Jesus told his disciples that some demons won't budge unless you fast and pray. Why did Jesus mention fasting? Surely, demons will respond to the name of Jesus, right? You don't need to fast to exorcise a demon, do you? Well, the big misunderstanding most people have when reading that scripture is they think Jesus was telling his disciples that fasting increases the anointing on your life, and that by increasing the anointing on your life you'll be able to cast out bigger and stronger demons. No. That's not what Jesus was saying. He was explaining to his disciples that they must fast not for more power, but so that they may have less flesh in the way when confronting certain spirits. Some spirits will begin to pull and feed on that which is inside of you before they give in. If they sense that you lack confidence in the name of Jesus, they'll feed on your unbelief. If they sense that you lack confidence in God's word, they'll feed on your unbelief. If they sense that you have sin which you've yet to repent of in your life, they'll feed on that. Like the demoniac in Acts chapter 19, some demons will look for weaknesses in you even while you're saying the name of Jesus. In that passage of scripture, the demon was bold enough to talk back to the seven exorcists, asking "I know Jesus, and I know Paul, but who are you?" If demons discover a small amount of residue from your past, they'll try to use it against you to derail you, shame you, and even destroy you; therefore, the fast is for the purpose of cleansing your spirit and your life of the residue and secret attachments that may still be clinging onto you. It is during our time of fasting that God reveals to us ties and attachments that need to be broken, and the power of our flesh is also broken in our lives.

EXERCISE:

This exercise will take more than a few seconds or minutes; it will take several days or weeks. I want you to take some time out of your busy schedule and fast. Now, there are books on fasting in Christian bookstores. I suggest you go and research this topic before doing it. There are many different types of fasts: some you can do while on medication, some you can do while working. Some fasts require that you eat no food whatsoever, some allow you to eat only fruits and vegetables (like the

Daniel Fast), and there's even one fast where you eat and drink nothing for a certain period of time. The extreme is a 40 day fast. Don't go beyond the limitations of your body. Start out light. Try once a week for half of a day. Or maybe take your lunch break and spend that time with God instead. May I suggest a partial fast starting out. Get used to fasting. The important thing about fasting is: while fasting, abstain not only from food (but do drink lots and lots of water and pure organic fruit juices. No sodas!), but you must definitely abstain from all forms of entertainment (TV, radio, etc.) that caters to the flesh. If you watch television or listen to the radio, it needs to be Christian programming you watch or listen to. But the best thing to do is put in a good worship CD and soak in the presence of God through praise and worship, and then spend a little time reading his word after your worship session.

As you fast, ask God to speak to you and reveal to you things you need to let go of. Ask him for discernment and wisdom. Ask him to cleanse your spirit man and get any residue from the "old man" out of you. And lastly, ask him to speak to you concerning his purpose for your life. When fasting, your spiritual senses are more alert. Your mind is clearer also. This is the prime time for God to speak to you. This is the prime time for you to hear his voice.

As God begins to speak to you, write down the things he reveals to you in your journal. He may speak softly into your spirit, give you a vision, a dream, or speak to you as you read his word. But whatever your spirit picks up, write it down. And after you write it down, pray over it some more.

PRAY THIS PRAYER:

Dear heavenly Father, I thank you for your love, mercy, and grace. I thank you for being my savior, my provider, and my protector. All good and perfect gifts come from you.

Dear Father, I come to you today with a heart of humility and repentance. Forgive me for any sins I may have committed against you. Cleanse my heart and mind of any spiritual contaminants that may rest inside of me. For you are the only one who can search the heart and expose what is in our souls. You know us through and through. We can hide nothing from you. So I ask, Father, that you would shine your glory upon me and expose everything in me that doesn't belong. Expose any hidden attachments and secret covenants I may have made with sin and demonic spirits, any and all soul ties I may have developed through sinful activities with others, and any secret contracts that may have been made with the enemy by my ancestors over my family bloodline. I break any ties to witchcraft, to Freemasonry, and to the occult over my life and over my family bloodline. I repent for reading horoscopes and playing with cursed objects. I divorce any and all secret idols in my life, whether it be persons, places or things. I release every loved one into your hands, and rebuke the spirit of grief that would seek to keep me bound to those who have passed away. Close every open door in my mind and heart which Satan and his demons may use to enter my life. Reveal to me any open doors in my home and life that may grant access to demonic spirits in my life and home. For, God, I will hold on to nothing you tell me to let go of. Expose the hand of the enemy in my life. Fill me with your truth, with your word, and with your Spirit so that I may be able to stand during my season of testing, so that Satan will find nothing in me that he can use. I give myself, my body, my soul, my spirit, my home, and my life to you. I am yours. And I thank you Father that as I consecrate more and more of myself to you, and even seek you through fasting, that you will begin to make clear to me the things I am to let go of, get rid of, and do. It is in Jesus name I pray, Amen.

PURPOSE SEEKERS

CHAPTER 5:
A NEW SEASON

*T*HERE ARE SOME THINGS THAT WILL COME whether or not you're ready for them. It doesn't matter if you believe in getting old or not—you cannot stay young forever. Wrinkles will come; gray hairs will grow; your steps will get slower. All of the Botox on the face of the planet won't hide age. The only thing you can do with age is...embrace it. Stop acting like a teenage girl when you're really a grandmother. Another thing we can't stop is death. As you've probably heard at many funerals: We will all be rolled down the aisle in a casket one day, so you better be ready when that day comes. It doesn't matter how much money you have, how many medical doctors you know, or how healthy you live; it's inevitable that you will one day leave this place. You can also count on your kids growing up and leaving you. It is scary when I look at my kids: it seems like it was only yesterday when they were little babies, and now they're so big. Pretty soon they won't be running into my room desiring to watch a family movie together. I know I will be begging them in a few short years just to spend time with me—their focus is going to shift to spending time with their friends and living in their own world. They'll also grow up and move on with their lives. They won't be cute little kids always. These are some of the things we can only prepare for—they can't be prevented from happening. Aside from these things there is another situation we can't prevent, but can only prepare for: the changing of seasons.

There are some seasons everyone is familiar with: summer, winter, spring and fall. With each season comes a different set of circumstances. For example, with summer comes hot weather, with winter comes cold weather; with spring comes pollen, bees, and new life; with fall comes cool weather and dying leaves. The days even get shorter during certain seasons (like during winter). Everything begins to change with a new season.

In the book of Ecclesiastes, Solomon lists several more seasons, many of which many people aren't familiar with. He wrote,

"For everything there is a season, and a time for every matter under heaven: a time to be born, and a time to die; a time to plant, and a time to pluck up what is planted; a time to kill, and a time to heal; a time to break down, and a time to build up; a time to weep, and a time to laugh; a time to mourn, and a time to dance; a time to cast away stones, and a time to gather stones together; a time to embrace, and a time to refrain from embracing; a time to seek, and a time to lose; a time to keep, and a time to cast away; a time to tear, and a time to sew; a time to keep silence, and a time to speak; a time to love, and a time to hate; a time for war, and a time for peace" (Ecclesiastes 3:1-8, English Standard Version).

I'm sure some of the seasons listed by Solomon sound a little harsh: a season where you have to kill, break down, weep, mourn, refrain from embracing, lose, keep silent, hate, and even go to war. Sure, it would be great if none of these things had to happen; if life was perfect, and we didn't have to prepare for bad situations; but the truth is we must learn to celebrate the good and expect the bad and not live blinded by unrealistic expectations. If good nations didn't go to war with bad nations, the world would fall under the control of evil men. In order for us to remain free as a nation, sometimes we have to fight those who want to destroy our nation—this means we must get on the battlefield and go to war. When we want to modernize our neighborhoods, we have to tear down old buildings. It doesn't matter if that old building was the popular spot back in the day. We have to let go of yesterday if we're going to move forward and build bigger and better things. I mean, who wants to be bothered with dial-up when they can get high speed internet through Comcast? And when we talk about things like weeping and mourning, no one wants to experience those things; but since loved ones pass on, pets die, our favorite clothes fade in color and become worn out, and our glorious yesterdays fade until out of view, we find ourselves weeping over the loss of these things while not realizing that we must lose in order to gain. Sometimes a loss prepares us to gain more. Sometimes losing money teaches us how to better handle money the next time we get some. God had to lose his son, Jesus, on the cross in order to gain millions of Christ-like Believers all over the world. And speaking of a time to refrain from embracing: my husband knows that there are times when I just need some space from him—just a little. I just need to get away and clear my head...then I'll be ready to be a wife and mother again. It is possible to smother people, even with affection. When you take a few moments just to do things apart, you will be excited to be around each other again when you do come back together. Knowing this, my husband started encouraging me to hang out with the ladies—to periodically do ladies night out. He would sense when I was feeling burnt out and needed a break from everything. *Kids will do it to you.* And boy, did I have to learn this one: there is a time to be quiet. It doesn't matter if you know you're right. You must learn to be quiet and let some people learn the hard way. If you don't let them learn, they will resent you and think that you're trying to control them. Sometimes, we wives are guilty of nagging our husbands: *you didn't do this; you didn't do that; you need to do this; you need to do that;* etc. I noticed one thing about my husband: when he is ready to do something, he'll do it; but when he doesn't feel like doing something, it doesn't matter what I say or how much I fuss, it won't get done. So, rather than fuss, I just do it myself. Sometimes, I'll start doing something myself and he will see me and feel guilty for letting me do it; he'll then step in and take over. I don't even have to say a word. All I have to do is let the Holy Spirit work on him. God will work on some people if you step out of the way.

SPIRITUAL SEASONS

Solomon talked about the natural seasons we experience in life, but there are even more seasons the Bible reveals to us in its pages: spiritual seasons. Unlike natural seasons where we're responsible for doing the sowing, spiritual seasons are designed to sow seed into us. These are the spiritual seasons: there is a season of testing, a season of blessings, a season of waiting, a season of serving, and a season to lead. The thing about each of these seasons is they each bring new challenges and skills into our lives. You must go through each season. If you try to skip one, you will miss the vital lessons meant for you to learn in order for you to fulfill God's purpose for your life. Let's examine these seasons a little closer.

There is a season of testing that must come to all of us as God's children. In Matthew chapter 4, Jesus was sent into the wilderness by the Holy Spirit to be tested by the devil. Notice that the Holy Spirit sent Jesus into the wilderness to face the devil. Sometimes God doesn't want you to rebuke pain and problems, he just wants you to trust him in them. God wants you to stand firm on your faith and continue to believe him despite how the situation looks. You can rebuke the storm over and over again until you turn blue in the face, but it won't go anywhere. It's not that God doesn't hear your prayers or that you aren't praying effectively; it's just that this is your season to be tested. The testing comes to reveal to you what is on the inside of you. Job continued to trust

God despite how things looked. And because Job didn't turn his back on God but continued to trust and praise God throughout his season of testing, God blessed him with double what he had before; and not only did God bless Job with double for his trouble, but God gave Job a level of authority with him that he didn't have before. Notice that God told Job after the trial that he would honor Job's request to either kill or spare the lives of his antagonizers. Authority in the spirit realm comes only after you've endured the tests and trials and have proven your love for God. This is why some men and women have been given more authority in the kingdom of God than others: they've endured certain tests and trials that earned them the right to be generals in the spirit. So, if you are going through something right now and you've prayed and prayed and prayed that it would leave but it hasn't left, then do as the Bible says in Hebrews 10:35-36 and keep hold of your "confidence" in Christ which brings great reward, and patiently wait for God to come through for you after you have done his will. It's not by your effort that God's promises will come to pass; it's by his power that they come to pass. All you can do at this point is sit still and remind yourself that God will come through; that's how you survive a season of testing. If, in your season of testing God reveals to you there is a lot of mess in your life that needs to come out, then continue to address the mess like we did in an earlier chapter and let God heal your heart. He's trying to purge and prune you so that you'll be ready for greater.

There are seasons of blessings that come our way. The season of blessings is the result of sowing into the kingdom of God during earlier times. In 2 Corinthians

9:6-11, Paul talked about the seed offering (the offering we give as a sacrifice to God out of appreciation for his gospel and saving grace. This offering is different from a tithe in that the tithe belongs to God automatically, but a seed offering is optional and must be an act of love). Paul wrote in verse eight that, as a result of sowing seed into the kingdom of God, God will supply favor to you so that you may prosper in your endeavors. Notice: Paul said that the amount of favor is determined by the size of your sacrifice in verse six. If you are a millionaire but you decide to sow a five dollar seed, then you will get a blessing that matches the size of you sacrifice—for a millionaire, five dollars is not a sacrifice. On the other hand, Jesus, in Luke chapter 21, commended the poor widow woman who gave two mites (a mite is the equivalent of a 10th of a penny) because that's all she had. She made a much bigger sacrifice in God's eyes because she gave all she had in the offering. God knows what's a true sacrifice for us, and he will challenge us accordingly. It's because of our sacrifices to God during these times that we reap blessings unexpectedly. And I want to remind you that every sacrifice is not a financial one. Along with financial sacrifices, we must sacrifice our time, sacrifice our dreams (as parents do when raising their children), and sacrifice many other things to serve God. God will bless us for our sacrifices. When you see someone blessed, don't focus on their glory and ignore their story. You don't know what they had to sacrifice in order for them to gain God's favor on their lives. The question is: Are you willing to make the same sacrifices?

The season of waiting can be a difficult one. This season can push you to your limit mentally. Sometimes, when a person is in their season of waiting they become impatient and feel the need to "help God out." This is what happened to Abraham: God promised him a child and then waited for over ten years before delivering the promise. Abraham and his wife, Sarah, grew impatient and started to question whether or not God was going to honor his promise made to them. Time seemed like the enemy. Years had gone by and Sarah was still childless. She was now in her nineties and it didn't seem as if God was going to come through for them. *Maybe he forgot,* Sarah and Abraham began to think to themselves. *Or perhaps God is waiting for us to help him in some way,* they thought. Their impatience led them to believe God needs man's help; they then concocted a plan to do so: Sarah suggested to her husband, Abraham, who by this time was around a hundred years old, to sleep with her maidservant, Hagar. Abraham didn't argue with her; he jumped right to it. Hagar conceived and bore a child: Ishmael. But as it turned out, Ishmael was not the child promised by God. When God finally did show up, he blessed Sarah's barren womb and allowed her to conceive and give birth to Isaac. It took the power of God in order for this to happen. When God makes us wait, it's usually because he's waiting for the circumstances to get so bleak that it will take a miracle for us to receive our breakthrough; that way, no one can take the credit for the blessing but God. But the important thing to do during this season is remind yourself of God's promises, and don't fall for the lie that God can't pull them off without your help—it's natural to think that, but God is not like man: his ways are higher than our ways. And more importantly, don't allow envy and jealousy to fill your heart. If you're not careful, you can end up looking at all of the people around you—at how they are being blessed—and start envying them. You can find yourself coveting what they have. The Bible says covetousness is really idolatry in Colossians 3:5. So, when you begin to desire someone else's blessing, you're making an idol out of their possessions. God desires to bless you, but his goal is to do it in such a way that it causes men's jaws to drop in amazement at how it happened. So, be careful how you conduct yourself when you feel as if God has placed you on a shelf. Be careful how you act when it is someone else's season to shine, and not yours. Just know that your miracle is in preparation; and that if you act a fool now, you'll end up looking and feeling silly later... just like Abraham and Sarah. Their impatience led to a dilemma, much heartbreak, and great shame.

The other season that comes our way is the season of serving. This is the season where we learn what it truly means to selflessly serve others without expecting anything in return from them. The critical lesson we're to learn during this season is humility. Humility is the key ingredient for a promotion according to 1 Peter 5:6-7. Those verses read: "Therefore humble yourselves [demote, lower yourselves in your own estimation] under the mighty hand of God, that in due time He may exalt you, casting the whole of your care [all your anxieties, all your worries, all your concerns, once and for all] on Him, for He cares for you affectionately and cares about you watchfully" (ESV). Peter mentioned in that same chapter that God "resists the proud" but "gives grace to the humble". If a person feels they're too big to humble themselves and become a servant, God will resist them (fight against them). Never think you're too big to serve others. Never think you're so important that everyone is supposed to be waiting on you at all times, and that you never have to wait on anyone...ever. If ever we do begin to think this way, God has a way of bringing us back to reality: he sends troubles our way that crush our pride. God does this with men who believe they're gods, with nations that think they're too prosperous to honor him and uphold his righteous standards, and with individuals who think they're too rich or too successful to think about him. A natural catastrophe is one way to remind all men, whether rich or poor, famous or unknown, that we need God. All of the money in the world can't save you when trapped beneath the rubble of an earthquake; nor can money, fame and prestige save you when facing a drought (shortage of food and water). All God is saying is "Don't get the big-head. I'm still in charge." God is the only one worthy of praise and glory. Pride makes men believe they should be worshiped, and pride is the very thing that landed Lucifer in hell. Pride is the thing that makes men believe they're too good to submit to another person's authority. But God tests us with authority. In Luke 16:10, Jesus says, "He that is faithful in that which is least is faithful also in much: and he that is unjust in the least is unjust also in much." What this means is: if you won't do your best in something because there isn't a large crowd present or because a certain someone isn't looking, then you're filled with pride. You're just waiting for a crowd so that you can be seen. You aren't serving; you're performing. A servant serves without seeking to be seen. Jesus also said in verse 12, "And if ye have not been faithful in that which is another man's, who shall give you that which is your own?" God may be testing you to see if you can fulfill another man's vision before he sends someone to help you fulfill your vision. When you take the attitude that you aren't going to give your all for someone else's company because you don't want to "make them rich," you're cutting your own blessing. What you don't realize is God will not send someone to bless your company because you selfishly refused to help another man obtain success. You reap what you sow. If you sow selfishness, you'll reap selfishness. Those who'll serve under you will have the same attitude you currently have towards your supervisor and boss. So many of us want God to bless us, but we aren't humble enough for him to bless us. We're too arrogant and defiant towards authority. We can't obey our parents as children, honor our husbands as wives, honor our spiritual coverings as Believers, and honor leadership in any other arena. This is a spirit of witchcraft/rebellion, and it must be broken before we can recieve God's blessings.

The last season in the spirit is the season to lead. After you learn to serve, you must learn to lead; in fact, the whole point of serving is to learn how to lead. When you sit under leaders, they'll show you how to be a great leader yourself. An humble spirit causes others to want to coach and mentor you and pour into you everything they have accumulated throughout the years which have led them to success. Mike Murdock calls this the *law of honor*. If we honor others, God will send people into our lives to honor us. God uses people to get us from one place to another in life. This is why we must learn how to follow and honor others: by doing so, God is able to align our lives with people who will favor us and bless us

beyond our wildest dreams; and while we're being blessed, others will be magnetically drawn to our lives simply
because they see the favor of God upon our lives. It's not
that they want to steal our favor and hold on to our coat
tails while we shoot towards the stars; it's that they want
to observe what we are doing to gain such favor. There is
a crowd waiting to observe your favor. There are people
you are meant to touch, to lead, to mentor. The blessing
of God on your life is not just for you; it's for others. If
you don't get this understanding, you'll undermine the
very purpose for the blessings of God in your life, which
is to gain the attention of others and make them hunger
after the God you serve. You are being the ultimate witness for Christ by allowing him to humble you, teach
you how to lead and to live a blessed life, and then bless
your socks off before the world's eyes. Some people will
never pay attention to your words; they will, however,
pay attention to your life. They'll watch you and follow
you from a distance without ever telling you. They don't
have to be in your face, stroking your ego with flattery
and praise; they're being impacted by you in total secret.
So understand that leadership is not about ego-tripping;
it's not about lording over people, which 1 Peter 5:1-5
warns against—as if you are God; it's about letting God
make an example out of you before others. People must
follow by choice, not by coercion and force; and for this
to happen, they must see something in—and on—your
life that attracts them.

CHANGING WEATHER

As I stated before, it's important to recognize differences
in seasons. Each season presents certain challenges to us,

which we must accomplish, and skills we must acquire; if you fail to pass that test, you may find yourself having to repeat that test all over again. If you don't gain humility, you will find yourself missing your promotion when the season to lead comes around. If you don't conquer the waiting season properly, you'll find yourself carrying spiritual babies into your next season that will become a hindrance to your progress: sins, habits, and people who become weights attached to you, dragging you down. If you fail during your season of testing, how can God ever trust you to survive outside of the wilderness. He'll have to keep you in the wilderness just as he did the children of Israel until he can mature you.

You will know your season is changing when two things begin to happen: you encounter new people who can help you get to the next level, and you acquire new revelations from God. These game-changers come at the end of a season, not the beginning; they come just after you've successfully passed your test; their task is to help you make the swift transition into the next season. Let's examine these two game-changers:

1. *The first change in weather is the arrival of God-sent people to coach and assist you into a new season.* The will of God for you entails new assignments, and each new assignment requires new people and skills. When it was time for Peter, James, John, Matthew, and the other disciples to fulfill their destinies, the heavenly Father sent Jesus. Had Jesus not come Peter's way, he would've never left that fishing boat and shook the world with the gospel message; Matthew would have remained behind that desk collecting taxes...and being despised. When it

was time for Elisha to walk in his destiny, God sent the prophet Elijah his way. When Paul's time came around, God sent Ananias his way to retrieve him from the side of the Damascus Road. And when God wanted to bless Paul's ministry, he sent a wealthy woman named Lydia to finance his ministry. Acts 16:14 says, "And a certain woman named Lydia, a seller of purple, of the city of Thyatira, which worshiped God, heard us: whose heart the Lord opened, that she attended unto the things which were spoken of Paul." Notice that God turned her heart towards Paul; that her decision to finance and support Paul's ministry was a divine arrangement. When God sends someone into our lives it's not because of our charming personalities or our ability to impress them; it's because of our purpose: they're attracted to the plan and purpose of God in our lives. I can remember when it was prophesied to me by a lady that God was going to send someone into my life to help me in ministry; that they'd genuinely care about me and would help armor-bear me. And it wasn't long after that a lady from my church came up to me and said God laid it on her heart to be my armor-bearer. She was certainly God-sent. It was later prophesied to me at a ministry that God was getting ready to shift my life and ministry to another level, and that he was going to send some very influential women into my life to get me to the place of my destiny. Shortly afterwards, the Holy Spirit laid it on my heart to hook up with a life coach who I had forgotten about. In prayer, he began showing me faces of people I had forgotten about. Each of these persons are responsible for me getting to the place I am at today.

The Bible says that when we give to God's house,

God will cause "men" to pour back into our bosoms in Luke 6:38. You can't get around people. Most individuals who don't like being around people are overcome by the fear of rejection. They are worried about how others perceive them; they're worried about being judged; and it is because of these fears they prefer to hide in a corner rather than go around others. But you must rebuke the spirit of fear and break the fear of rejection through the power of the Holy Spirit so that you can open yourself up to the blessings of God which he intends to deliver to you through others.

The Bible says your gift will make room for you and bring you before great men in Proverbs 18:16. This is what happened to Daniel and Joseph: their spiritual gifts brought them before kings. The reason God wants to bring you before great people is so that he can position you in a place of greatness for his glory and purpose. Esther's beauty put her in a position to become the Queen of Persia; and God put her in that position "for such a time as this" (Esther 4:14): a time when the Jews needed someone to represent them in the royal palace and convince the Persian king to stop the Jewish people from being annihilated at the hands of Persia's Prime Minister, Haman. The positioning of Esther in that kingdom wasn't an accident, just like the timing of your birth and the gifts of God in your life are no accidents or coincidences. The people in your life aren't there by accident or coincidence either. If you came out of a crazy household, your experiences are the tools God is using to shape your ministry. Your pain becomes your passion, and your passion will become your ministry. You can witness to drug addicts effectively because you use to be one. You can relate to troubled teens a lot easier than others because you were one. You can have compassion on the lost because you use to be lost. Don't rule out the blessings that negative situations can bring your way. God can use anyone to bless and position you in life, but you must trust him and walk in forgiveness.

The key to getting God to send people into your life to guide you into your destiny is: seeking to please God and not people. Place all of your focus on God and pursuing him, and he'll "add" everything you need—including the right people—to your life. In Proverbs 16:7, God tells us, "When a man's ways please the LORD, he maketh even his enemies to be at peace with him." *Hear that?* God will bless you even through people that don't like you...when you focus on pleasing him rather than pleasing them. Hold on to your standards in Christ. Don't lower your standards for others. Continue to be kind to others. Be loving, but don't compromise in order to fit in with others. Let those who will leave, leave. In John 6:59-65, the Bible tells us that over 70 disciples of Jesus abandoned him after misinterpreting a statement of his. Everyone can't follow you to where God is taking you. Stop trying to make everyone follow you, and stop worrying about those who won't support you. After, and only after, you surrender to Christ, your purpose, and not your personality, will determine who comes into your life. That may even include a Judas.

Proverbs 15:22 says, "Without counsel purposes are disappointed: but in the multitude of counselors they are established." According to Proverbs, we all need counselors when we have a vision or a plan. If we try to do things on our own, Solomon says we'll only end up with frustration and disappointment. You can't accomplish God's purpose alone, so he sends people your way.

2. *The second change in weather is the acquisition of new revelations from God.* By revelations, I am talking about the understanding of God's word. Jesus explained to his disciples in John 16:12-14, "I still have many things to say to you, but you cannot bear them now. When the Spirit of truth comes, he will guide you into all the truth, for he will not speak on his own authority, but whatever he hears he will speak, and he will declare to you the things that are to come. He will glorify me, for he will take what is mine and declare it to you." The level of our maturity in God determines the level of revelation he gives us. Everyone is not spiritually mature enough to handle what God really desires to tell them, to chew on strong meat. Everyone is not interested in this book's subject matter: they haven't arrived at the place in their lives where truth interests them; they are not tired of living life their way; they don't want to face the truth of where they are spiritually; they don't want to face the reality of their soul's condition. God desires to share revelations with us that will change our lives and thrust us forward into the next level of his purpose for us, but we must be prepared to hear what he has to say. This is why we must attend Bible study, read God's word daily, and meditate upon his word. The more we read his word, the more God speaks to us through his word. God works with his word.

According to 2 Timothy 2:15, by applying ourselves to the dilligent study of God's word, we reveal to God our readiness and willingness to be used by him in a greater capacity. The flip side of that is: by not applying ourselves to the study of God's word, we show a lack of readiness and our unwillingness to be used by God in a greater capacity—or used by him at all.

In Hosea 4:16, God stated: "My people are destroyed for lack of knowledge; because you have rejected knowledge, I reject you from being a priest to me. And since you have forgotten the law of your God, I also will forget your children" (ESV). God said we are destroyed because of what we don't know. Ignorance isn't bliss. If you don't know you are living in sin, that ignorance will cost you your soul. If you don't know right from wrong you will end up doing that which brings eternal damnation and judgment upon you. For example, in Jeremiah 4:22, God stated the reason he had to judge his own people, the Israelites. He said, "For my people is foolish, they have not known me; they are sottish (foolish) children, and they have none understanding: they are wise to do evil, but to do good they have no knowledge." The Israelites became so ignorant of God's word they no longer knew the difference between right and wrong—that means they committed murder while thinking it wasn't wrong, they lied on one another while thinking it was alright; they stole, coveted, and cheated without feeling any type of conviction. When a person chooses not to become knowledgeable of God's word (which reveals his ways, desires, likes, and dislikes), God will reject them. If we don't know God's ways, we will misrepresent him where ever we go; and if we can't represent God, he can't afford to position us in places of influence.

There are many people in the world today who are knowledgeable of everything but the word of God.

They know about politics, science, business and history, but they can't quote any Bible. Some people can quote every lyric to every rap or secular song, but not a single Bible verse...besides Psalm 23 and John 3:16. But God said in Hebrews 6:1-3, "So let us stop going over the basic teachings about Christ again and again. Let us go on instead and become mature in our understanding. Surely we don't need to start again with the fundamental importance of repenting from evil deeds and placing our faith in God. You don't need further instruction about baptisms, the laying on of hands, the resurrection of the dead, and eternal judgment. And so, God willing, we will move forward to further understanding" (NLT). And then God went on to state that those who misrepresent him before the world are "nailing him to the cross once again and holding him up to public shame" (vs. 6, NLT). We must graduate to the next level of maturity in our understanding of God's word before he blesses us with next level blessings and uses us for his purpose. You must know what grade you're in in the spirit; or as Paul wrote, "Because of the privilege and authority God has given me, I give each of you this warning: Don't think you are better than you really are. Be honest in your evaluation of yourselves, measuring yourself by the faith God has given us" (Romans 12:3, NLT).

There is a war going on between our flesh and our spirit. The Bible tells us there is no good thing in our flesh in Romans 7:18. That's why it's always a fight just to do what's right. Satan doesn't want you to graduate to the next level of understanding in God's word. He will do whatever it takes to distract you. Have you ever noticed that when it's time to go to a birthday party or a celebration you suddenly get a ton of energy, even after you've worked all day—you will make time to hang out and have fun; you'll even get creative with your fashion, hair, etc., making sure everything is on point. But when it's time to pray, read your Bible, or even go to church, you'll suddenly feel tired. Or how about when it's time to hear and receive the teaching of the word: you all of a sudden find yourself getting sleepy. Some people get their best sleep when the word is being ministered. They don't sleep while the choir is up. Sleep only comes over them when it's time to hear the word.

WHEN SOMETHING BEGINS TO STINK

One day, I went to the grocery store and bought some salmon to cook for the family. I remember cooking it and then getting so busy after dinner with other things that I forgot to put the rest up. As days went by, I started smelling a foul smell; it was fuming up the entire house. I began freaking out. I cleaned the entire house, but still couldn't target where the smell was coming from. But I did begin to notice that the smell was very strong in the kitchen area. I started moving stuff around, picking up and smelling everything; suddenly, I noticed a white paper bag tucked away behind our George Foreman griller on the kitchen counter. When I opened it a foul smell hit me: it was the salmon I bought days earlier. It had turned spoil. I thought to myself, "How can something that tastes so good end up smelling so bad?" The reality of seasons is: some people and things are meant only for that season, but not for the next. It's easy to get attached to the people and things God brings into our lives for a certain season, but forget that they aren't meant to stay in our lives forever. When we forget that some of the people God sends us are seasonal, we become offended when they leave us; we may even feel they've abandoned us when, really, it was just time for them to leave. If you try to keep them around, they might start to spoil...and stink up your life. The same is said when we take food into our bodies. If we don't detox our bodies, the food in our systems will turn into poison and produce toxins inside of us. These toxins will take a tole on your health, making you sick. In order to feel better, you will need to get rid of the toxins that are stored up in your body. There comes a time when we all need to spiritually examine our lives and get rid of the old stuff we've stored up and held on to for too long, stuff that has out-served its purpose and outlived its season in our lives. What is it that we are holding on to that is blocking us from moving forward? Why are we holding on to the past so tightly? Are you continuing to think the way you did in the past rather than embrace the change of mind God is trying to give you? Don't allow outdated stuff to produce toxins in your spirit and life. Let go when God says let go, and move on when God says move on.

In Numbers chapter 21, God commanded Moses to create a brass serpent and place it on a pole so that all who looked upon it would be healed from the venom from the poisonous snakes God sent into the camp as a punishment for their constant bickering and complaining. The brass serpent worked for the time being, but it outlived its purpose after that season was over. Unfortunately, the Israelites couldn't realize when it was time to embrace something new; so they turned the brass snake into an idol and began worshipping it. God said that he desires to do a new thing, and that he wants us to forget about the old things in Isaiah 42:9. Don't live in the past, lest the past becomes your idol. Paul said in Philippians that he considered his past accomplishments to be "dung," and that he was focused on the "mark of the high calling" of Christ that was before him in Philippians 3:14. Focusing on what God has in front of you will help you forget about what is behind you.

God has a bright future in front of you. His plan and purpose for your life is so bright that yesterday can't even compare. Paul said in Romans chapter 8 that your future glory is far greater than the sufferings of the present. So look ahead. Follow the dream God placed inside of you. Walk out the purpose he has for you one season at a time. Expect to be great, to do great things, and to leave a lasting impact on many. It's your destiny.

EXERCISE:

Take a look at the present. Ask God to reveal to you what season he has you in. Ask God to reveal to you the things he wants you to learn in this season. While spending time in prayer and reading God's word, write down the things God tells you as he speaks to you. Work on those areas in your life you know God is dealing with you in. If you don't know how to serve, work on being a better servant. If you have trouble being patient and waiting on God, work on being patient and not being ruled by anxiety. If God is calling you to leadership, step up to the plate and do what he is calling you to do in this hour.

While examining your life, take inventory of the things in your life: friends, relationships (besides family since family will always be a responsibility of ours), jobs, careers, old skill sets, methods, ways, settings, practices, etc. Ask God to remove the things out of your life that are hindrances to your purpose, and send the individuals and things into your life that are meant to operate in your life in this season. Ask God to give you the wisdom and the strength to cut loose those things which do not belong in your life. Ask God to empty your spirit of any toxins (toxic thinking) that have developed inside you. This is the time to let old things go and embrace the new work and things he is bringing into your life. Do this exercise in your journal.

PRAY THIS PRAYER:

Dear heavenly Father, I come to you today thanking you for your presence, and for all of your wonderful blessings. I thank you that you saved me, brought me into your kingdom, gave me a new name and identity, and endowed me with power and purpose. I thank you for working out your plans for my life. For it is you who is orchestrating the events of my life so that I will walk in your perfect will for me.

Father, I thank you for the season you have me in. I thank you for the wisdom and discernment to know what season I'm in. Teach me what I need to know during this season. Teach me how to humble myself, how to put others before me, how to lead by example, how to wait on you and not get impatient and anxious, how to reap the blessings you have in store for me, how to sow in order that I might have a harvest to reap, how to conduct my self with wisdom in every situation, how to let go of things that are out-dated in my life, and how to embrace the changes you are bringing into my life. I thank you for the strength and anointing to break and sever every destructive tie to people and past events that are hindering me from moving forward in you. Let me get a glimpse of the future you have for me so that I will forget the past and let go of past glories. For your plans are bright for me. It doesn't matter what age I am or where I am in life; your plans are to bless me, and not to curse me; to give me an expected end. Today, I receive it. Today, open my eyes to greater revelations from your word. Teach me your ways, and how to please you. Give me a heart of understanding and wisdom, and the mind of Christ. Open my spiritual eyes as I read your word. Let revelations from your word flood my soul as I read your word. Give me discernment to know when I am being taught the truth, or when someone is leading me in the spirit of error. Holy Spirit, you are called the Spirit of Truth in 1 John chapter 4. You are my eternal guide and companion. Today, I am ready to receive that which you have for me. Grow me up spiritually. Mature me so that I may go on to greater revelations and greater works for the kingdom of God. I thank. It's in Jesus name I pray, Amen.

CHAPTER 6:
STEP INTO THE FLOW

*I*N CHRIST WE LIVE AND BREATHE and have our being. In Christ there is no condemnation. In Christ we can do all things. It's only *in* Christ...

We can do everything in our power to make our lives prosperous: we can get all of the degrees, befriend every person we think has connections, go to every business meeting in town, etc., but in the end what matters most is whether or not you're *in* God's favor. Don't let others fool you. Some people may say, "I don't need God. I can prosper without him." Well, to this, Jesus responded that a fool is one who stores "up earthly wealth but not have a rich relationship with God" (Luke 12:21, NLT). Being rich towards God is a matter of having his favor and storing up eternal wealth in heaven. Jesus also went on to say, "...That is why I tell you not to worry about everyday life—whether you have enough food to eat or enough clothes to wear. For life is more than food, and your body more than clothing" (Luke 12:21-23, NLT). He was explaining that we should never worry about these things because God will take care of us when we seek after him. Earlier in that same chapter, Jesus explained: "Beware! Guard against every kind of greed. Life is not measured by how much you own" (vs. 15). Most people who claim to be successful only have stuff, and not life. They aren't living out their destinies; they're just existing, counting down the days to the inevitable: their death. And when they die, their souls, not being prepared because they were into stuff and not into Christ, will certainly find themselves separated eternally from God...and heaven. The emptiness of purpose-less living and the bland routine of buying more stuff just to temporarily satisfy your insatiable flesh is not living.

In Christ we find life, and life more abundantly; but this abundant life of ours is "hid with Christ" Paul stated in Colossians 3:3. I can remember playing hide-and-go-seek when I was a little girl. The objective was to find the person who was hiding; or, if you were the one hiding, avoid being found. It was a fun game centered around adventure—around searching to find someone. You couldn't just sit still and expect the person to come out of hiding and jump into your lap. You had to set out on a hunt...and go looking. God hides our destinies so that we'll go looking for them, and he lets us know that there's no need to look for them anywhere else (in loved ones, friends; other people, places, and things) because our destinies are hidden...inside of Christ. It's inside of Jesus the Christ we find all we need.

How do we step into Christ? The first and obvious answer, of course, is to submit our lives to him and accept him as lord and savior; in other words: get saved. But there's more to this puzzle than merely praying the *sinner's prayer*. Many church goers, after confessing Jesus as lord and savior, still don't know how to walk "in" Christ. Paul said to the church in Rome, "Therefore we are buried with him (Christ) by baptism into death: that like as Christ was raised up from the dead by the glory of the Father, even so we also should walk in newness of life" (Romans 6:4). He also wrote in Romans 8:1, "There is therefore now no condemnation to them which are in Christ Jesus, who walk not after the flesh, but after the Spirit." Notice that the emphasis is on walking after the Holy Spirit—learning to follow the Holy Spirit. Only he can help you walk in Christ. Lastly, Paul said, "As ye have therefore received Christ Jesus the Lord, so walk ye in him" (Colossians 2:6). The point Paul is trying to get across to Believers is this: don't simply profess to be saved and then stop there, but acquire the skills needed to deepen your relationship with Christ, and also learn how to pursue after Christ. As Paul wrote in Philippians 3:12, "Not as though I had already attained, either were already perfect: but I follow after, if that I may apprehend that for which also I am apprehended of Christ Jesus." Paul was explaining to us that the Christian walk is like a game of tag: God catches us first then he tags us; then it's our turn to chase after him, catch, and tag him. Christ apprehended us, now we must pursue him daily in an attempt to apprehend him. A purpose seeker is a God chaser.

OPPORTUNITIES ARE WAITING

Many people give up on themselves due to factors such

as age, disability, lack of education, lack of finances, lack of support from family and friends, and failed attempts. They begin to feel as if God can't use them, or their time has passed. They think they've missed too many opportunities to do and be something great, and then they settle for mediocrity just like Rapunzel did in our earlier chapter for much of her life. But the misunderstanding they have regarding the will of God is this: our purposes in life are our God-given assignments; our assignments bring with them every divine resource that we need to successfully accomplish them—the people, favor, blessings, wisdom, skills, etc. But, though it's easy to assume that God has enough people available to do his will in the earth, it's actually the opposite. Jesus said, "The harvest is plenteous, but the laborers are few; Pray ye therefore the Lord of the harvest, that he will send forth laborers into his harvest" (Matthew 9:38). What Jesus was saying is: there is more work to be done than people willing and available to do it. When I say that most people tend to slip into a mode of mediocrity, I mean people tend to overlook the work that must be done in order to win the lost for Christ and they simply focus on trying to survive until they expire (die). They have turned their backs on the adventurous call of evangelism, of pushing God's agenda and will in the earth, of tearing down the kingdom of darkness and snatching lost souls from the hands of the enemy. There are so many places where the gospel needs to go, so many souls that need to hear the gospel, so many souls on their way to a burning hell, so many assignments that don't have willing participants to complete them, so many mantles and anointings that are sitting in heaven's storage room that God is waiting to release to individuals that are willing to be used by him; there's too much to do for you to sit back and lick the wounds of yesterday, talking about what you missed or wish you could've done. That's the problem: you're living for you, not God's will. Find a place in the field and get busy. Also, while laboring in the vineyard, pray for God to open the eyes of more sleeping Christians and let them see the amount of work they're missing out on while they're sitting back licking their wounds or focusing on gratifying self. That is why Paul said in Ephesians 5:14, "...Awake thou that sleepest, and arise from the dead, and Christ shall give thee light (revelation)." He then said, "See then that ye walk circumspectly, not as fools, but as wise, redeeming the time, because the days are evil. Wherefore be ye not unwise, but understanding what the will of the Lord is" (vs. 15-17). Since the days are overrun by evil, we don't have time to be distracted. We have to become wise to the will of God in the earth, that will being to win the lost...not bless you to become complacent with a four bedroom house in a gated community. God isn't calling you to comfort, but to kingdom work. People are not suffering from missed opportunities; but rather, opportunities are suffering from missing people. Everyday of your life opportunities to do God's will are all around you. Are you plugging into God so that you can be led by his Spirit into one of the billions of assignments that are sitting right before your eyes? Everyday, you must ask God to use you, to show you opportunities to accomplish his will in the earth. Ask God to open the doors, give you the words to say, set up the contacts, set up the circumstances, and send the anointing; and keep in mind that you're focusing on doing his will and not your own. Remember: when we focus on God's will, God will focus on our circumstances. Put God first and he will make you his priority. Put selfish desires first and God will turn his attention elsewhere.

There are no missed opportunities in the kingdom of God. If you feel as if there was an assignment you were supposed to do for God but didn't accomplish it due to fear or being distracted, the good news is there are millions of others where that came from. Satan will trick you into remaining focused on the opportunities you missed in order to distract you from the opportunities coming your way. No one's perfect. No one hits the bullseye each and every time. Just know that opportunities will never cease, so you shouldn't quit. I don't care if you're in prison; you have an opportunity to impact and change the lives of those who society has forgotten. You're still in a great position to serve God's will. There's someone waiting for you; God has something for you to give to them: a word of revelation that will change their life, a word of prayer that will break demonic bondages off of them, a word of encouragement that will prevent them from taking their life, or simply a helping hand to walk with them as they journey into their destiny. Make yourself useful and quit wasting time licking wounds.

JUMP IN THE WATER

In John chapter 5, there's a story of a man that was paralyzed, laying by a pool called Bethesda. It was believed that every so often an angel would descend into the waters of the pool and then stir them; and anyone who was sick, if they jumped into the pool while the waters were being stirred, would be healed. This man sat by this pool for 38 years waiting for someone to help him into the waters so that he could get his healing. He couldn't find anyone to help him. One day Jesus approached him and asked him if he wanted to be made whole. The man responded with a series of excuses, explaining why he was still sick, blaming others for his situation. Jesus didn't want to hear the excuses; he wanted to know if the man was ready for a change of circumstances. So, Jesus asked him to take a step of faith and pick up his own bed and walk with it. Acting on the instructions of Christ, the man began moving his limbs. As he moved them in an attempt to obey Jesus' instruction, he noticed they were gaining strength. He finally stood up and picked up his bed as Jesus commanded him to do. It's easy to make excuses when God is calling us, to explain to him why we can't seek his face and answer his call; but God doesn't want to hear excuses, he only wants you to take a step of faith and do what he says. Excuses rob us of our ability to live the life God wants us to live. Don't constantly tell yourself what you can't do; tell yourself what you can do through Christ's power.

The man was waiting to step into the water as it was being stirred by the angel, but Jesus was giving him the opportunity to step into the *living water* sitting before him—to step into the faith-zone. God is always near, and we must learn to step into him. We must jump into the current of the Holy Spirit's presence and allow ourselves to be swept away; to walk by faith, and not by sight. Faith doesn't mean "belief"; but rather, "hearing and obeying God's instructions." We must step into the flow of God's Spirit in order to receive our assignments, receive revelations, receive strength, find purpose, and discover who we are. We step into the flow of the Holy Spirit every time we do these things:

1. *Enter into our prayer closets and spend time with God.* Jesus taught us to enter into our prayer closets when we get ready to pray. The prayer closet is a metaphor for a state of mind: we must seek God privately and sincerely, not for the purpose of showing off in front of people. There are corporate prayers and private prayers—a time to pray corporately with other Believers, and a time to seek God all by yourself. Jesus says we must learn to seek God in private even before praying corporately. When we call on God in private and with a sincere heart, Jesus said God will reward us openly in Matthew 6:6.

2. *Seek God before doing anything else.* Many times we'll run to God in the morning and toss him a laundry list of problems to attend to as if giving him an assignment... like we're his boss. This isn't the definition of spending time with God. Spending time with God means forgetting about the world and jumping into his presence. This requires time. You have to set aside time for God and don't treat him like he's not worth the sacrifice. David said in Psalm 63:1, "O God, thou art my God; early will I seek thee: my soul thirsteth for thee..." David would designate time early in the morning before the day began, while his mind was clear and fresh; he didn't wait until the middle of the day, or the end of the day, after his mind had grown cluttered by all of the challenges and problems he faced. The time to pray is before problems hit, not after they hit. If we pray first, before

we start our day, God can give us a strategy to deal with the problems waiting for us or cause us to avoid them.

Don't let the television or telephone steal God's time in the morning. Don't run out of the front door in the morning without having consecrated your day to God. How you start your day determines how your day goes. Practice making this a habit over the next 30 days.

3. *Press into the presence of God through praise and worship*. The flesh never desires to press into God's presence. It doesn't want you to pray at all, but it will tolerate you giving God 30 seconds of your time...and no more. But your flesh (carnal nature) will never tolerate you seeking God through intense worship. When in real worship we forget about problems, things, and ourselves; we end up being saturated by the glorious presence of God.

The Bible says in Psalm 100:4, we are to "enter his gates with thanksgiving and his courts with praise." A big part of worship is thanking God for his blessings and his presence. Everyone has something to be thankful for, but the biggest reason we thank God is because he showed us his love in that he sent his own son, Jesus, to die for us on the cross and bear our sins on his back. After thanking God, we begin to praise him for who he is. We declare his wonderful works, his glory; that he is holy, excellent, mighty and majestic. The same way you praise someone in order to build them up, you praise God because he is worthy. God is worthy of praise not because of what he does, but because of who he is. The President of the United States receives special recognition because of his office. God deserves special recognition because of his office: he's God, the creator of heaven and earth, the beginning and the end; the sovereign, omniscient, omnipotent and omnipresent creator. That means he is deserving of more recognition, honor, and praise than any man or anything in existence. We owe God praise. Would you bless someone who's ungrateful, who wouldn't even thank you for the things you gave to them before, and who disrespects and dishonors you? If you wouldn't do anything else for them because of their lack of respect and gratitude, then how do you think God feels when we go to him simply demanding things but won't even take any time out to be grateful for all of the things he has already done for us? He feels the same way you'd feel.

If you're going to enter into the flow of worship, it is important that you remove distractions and get into a place where you can focus on God alone. Go to another room in the house and shut the door. Go to the car and shut the door. Designate a special place where you and God can share that time together. After you go to that special place, put on some worship music. I love to listen to Kim Walker-Smith, Juanita Bynum, and other worshippers. Their music helps me to take the focus off of me and put it on God. I don't advise listening to music that focuses on you. Worship is about God, not you. Some songs are good for the purpose of encouraging you when going through your storms, but they are not meant for worship. Music that speaks about God's glory, his majesty, that places all of the focus and attention on him, that commands your spirit to hunger and thirst for God's presence is music that's meant for worship.

3. *Pray in the Spirit.* In 1 Corinthians 14:18, Paul said, "I

thank my God, I speak with tongues more than ye all..."
Paul confessed that one of his regular routines in the
morning—and also throughout the day—was to pray in
tongues, which is an unknown heavenly language given
to us by God. Tongues is not the sign that you are saved;
it is, however, a sign that the Holy Spirit dwells within
you. It is possible to receive a gift from the Holy Spirit
and then backslide, thereby keeping the gift but losing
fellowship with God according to Romans 11:29. But
it is also important to remember that spiritual gifts first
come from the Holy Spirit according to 1 Corinthians
chapter 12. So, the administering of gifts and offices is
done by the Holy Spirit, not the flesh. You can't receive
one of the spiritual gifts listed in 1 Corinthians chapter
12 through time, age, and experience.

There are various types of tongues: some can be
interpreted by others—they're usually spoken in earthly
languages which man can understand—and there are
tongues which no man can understand, and these are a
language understood only by God. Romans 8:26 talks
about the Holy Spirit helping us to pray by causing us to
utter "groanings which cannot be uttered". We cannot
understand what we are saying, but God can. Although
human understanding is in the dark, according to Paul
in 1 Corinthians 14:2, "...one who speaks in a tongue
speaks not to men but to God; for no one understands
him, but he utters mysteries in the Spirit" (ESV). We're
praying mysteries when we speak in tongues. We're declaring things in the spirit God desires to establish upon
this earth. We're supernaturally praying God's will.

The gift of tongues not only causes you to pray
deep mysteries into existence, but it also stirs your spirit

up. In Jude, verse 20, the author says, "But ye, beloved, building yourselves on your most holy faith, praying in the Holy Ghost..." When we pray in the Spirit we build up our spirits—we stir our spirits, thereby causing other gifts to be stirred. If you cook a pot of grits and leave it sitting out for a long time, the grits will harden; but if you continuously stir the grits, they will remain loose... and be more edible. Some of us have treasures, gifts and other things stuck in our spirits that need to be stirred up in the Holy Ghost; we, therefore, need to pray in the Spirit to stir them up. Many great men and women of God who did extraordinary things in life for the glory of God attributed their success to one thing: they would pray in tongues daily, usually for an hour or more. They started their day in the presence of God, with the Spirit of God, praying in the Spirit; and because of this, they were able to operate in the heart of God and walk in the flow of the Spirit of God. The Holy Spirit could speak to them and tell them where to go, who to talk to, what to say, who to give to, how to dress that morning, what to do in a certain situation, etc. They were in the flow.

It's time for you to step into the flow. Get into the presence of God and get in sync with his will. Allow the Holy Spirit to operate in you at a greater capacity than he is right now. The more you surrender your body to God as a living sacrifice, the more the Holy Spirit can invade your life and take complete control of it.

IT'S TIME TO DIE

In Galatians 3:1-5, Paul rebuked the Christians in the church in Galatia for abandoning the Holy Spirit and relying on the flesh in order to accomplish God's will for them. Paul explained to them—and us—that you can't begin the journey into God's purpose for your life in the Spirit and then try to finish it using your own intellect, smarts, networking, and carnal understanding. God is teaching you in this hour how to rely on him and him alone for everything. Sure, you can do what others are doing who don't know God, but that's not the way God desires for your life to go. He wants to teach you how to depend on him completely. He wants you to turn to him for everything, big and small. He wants to get all of the credit and glory in your life. He's looking for you to be his ambassador in the earth. That's why he wants you to die to your will, to your ways, and "lean not to your own understanding," but in everything acknowledge him, and then he will begin to direct your path. Die to *self* today and let God have his way with you.

PRAY THIS PRAYER:

Dear heavenly Father, I thank you for your grace, your mercy, and your love. You have been better to me than I have been to myself. You are so wonderful to me, and I want to thank you before I do or say anything else. I am alive today because of your grace, and I exist to serve your will and purpose in the earth. So, I give you myself today. I give you my body as a living sacrifice. Wash it, cleanse it with your blood, make me holy and acceptable in your sight. I have no righteousness outside of you. You are my righteousness. It's in you that I am whole, that I am complete, that I am victorious

---

over the world and the works of Satan, that I have joy, peace, love, power, patience, self-control, wisdom, understanding, deliverance, healing, and a purpose. Outside of you I am nothing. I totally depend on you for everything, and your guidance in every situation. I choose not to look to myself for guidance, but I look to you Holy Spirit to be my guide, my comforter, my ultimate counselor, and my friend. I thank you for your guidance. Forgive me Holy Spirit if I have grieved you in any way. Forgive me if I have disrespected you or tempted you in any way. Teach me to be ever so aware of your presence at all times. Teach me how to honor your presence, how to commune with you, how to hear your voice, how to be sensitive to your gentle Spirit, how to follow you, and how to obey you. Holy Spirit, I thank you that by faith you promised to fill all who are thirsty. Today, I am thirsty for your presence. My soul is thirsty for more of you. I thank you that you have already saved me, but now I desire that you fill me, Holy Spirit. By faith, I receive the in-filling of the Holy Spirit in my life with the gift of speaking in tongues. I thank you Father for giving me the gift of the Holy Spirit and for giving me my prayer language. Today, I receive it. Holy Spirit, give me utterance as only you can. Lead me as only you can. Let me operate in your divine will, in your heart, heavenly Father. I thank you. I pray this prayer, in Jesus name, Amen.

Final Word

GOD HAS THE MASTER PLAN. He created you for his purpose, and not your own. Realize that God has the plan for your life—that map we talked about at the beginning of the book—in the palm of his hand, and he is anxious to work through you to execute it.

It's all about God. He designs us in our mothers' wombs, endows us with purpose, draws us by his Holy Spirit, and empties us of ourselves—our dreams, aspirations, hopes, desires, and understanding—then replaces these things with his dreams and aspirations, hopes, desires, and the mind of Christ so that we may walk in his wisdom and understanding. What can you give God? A talent? Where do you think that talent came from? Money? How can you bribe God with money when he uses gold as pavement in heaven? There's nothing you can give him...but an empty vessel, one that's willing to let him execute within and through it a plan he created, a plan that's too big for human effort, one that takes his power to bring to pass. What God desires to do through you is bigger than just you.

The dream God wants to give you is so big that it will take him to bring it to pass. He just needs you to dream it, declare it, and then let him miraculously bring it into manifestation. But it has to be his dream and not yours. God doesn't want you believing in yourself. That is the problem to begin with. You don't have the ability to know the mind of God in your flesh, neither do you have the ability to execute the plans of God for your life through your flesh. God wants you believing and relying solely on him. And, perhaps, he's teaching you to do so in this season. That's why your plans aren't working, and your methods aren't fruitful. God has to let you get exhausted before you'll finally give up and turn to him.

It's during intimate times with God that he will begin to give you a dream that's bigger than you. And he will also guide you every step of the way into his plan as you continue to seek after him. Let your lifestyle be that of a God seeker: a person who's in constant pursuit of God's presence. And as you pursue after God, he will guide you step by step, day by day, into *his* purpose for you. You were born for it. You were destined for it. You were created to be an example of what God can do with a man, a woman, who yields to God. Let God make you that example today. Be the clay in his hands, the vessel in his possession, the tool he uses to liberate those who are captive to sin and satanic bondage, the person whose life serves the true purpose for which it was established on the earth: to bring glory to his name.

Let us pray:

Dear heavenly Father, I thank you for all that you have done and are doing in my life. I thank you for what you are getting ready to do in and through me as well. You have great plans for my life, and that's why I am yielding my life to you today. Work your plans, your will through me. I am yours. Have your way in me today.

Father, let your desires penetrate my heart, and fill my mind. I surrender my heart, mind, body and soul to you so that you may fill me up completely. I know that you are a big God and you want to do a big work in and through me. So, I remove me out of the way so that you may do in and through me whatever you desire to do. I say yes to you today.

Thank you. It is in Jesus name I pray, Amen.

CPSIA information can be obtained at www.ICGtesting.com
Printed in the USA
LVOW07s2006160714

394589LV00002B/4/P